Truths that Build

Principles that Will Establish

and Strengthen the People of God

DICK IVERSON

CITY BIBLE
PUBLISHING

Portland, Oregon, U.S.A.

PUBLISHED BY CITY BIBLE PUBLISHING

9200 NE Fremont, Portland, Oregon 97220

Printed in U.S.A.

City Bible Publishing is a ministry of City Bible Church and is dedicated to serving the local church and its leaders through the production and distribution of quality restoration materials.

It is our prayer that these materials, proven in the context of the local church, will equip leaders in exalting the Lord and extending His kingdom.

For a free catalog of additional resources from City Bible Publishing please call 1-800-777-6057 or visit our website at www.citybiblepublishing.com.

Truths that Build

International Standard Book Number: 1-886849-80-3

All scripture quotations, unless otherwise indicated, are taken from the Authorized King James Version.

Other versions used are:

The Amplified Bible – Copyright © 1958 by Zondervan Publishing. Used by Permission. All Rights Reserved.

NKJV – New King James Version. Copyright © 1982 by Thomas Nelson, Inc. Used by permission. All rights reserved.

Library of Congress Cataloging-in-Publication Data

Iverson, Dick.
 Truths that build : principles that will establish and strengthen
the people of God / Dick Iverson.
  p. cm.
 ISBN 1-886849-80-3 (pbk. : alk. paper)
 1. Christian life. I. Title.
BV4501.3 .I94 2001
248.4–dc21
            2001004392

Dedication

I wish to dedicate this series of messages to the most important people in my life, my family. Their support throughout my life is immeasurable.

My wife Edie has walked with me for over fifty years of marriage. She is a true woman of God and a giant when it comes to faith.

I feel the same way about my four wonderful daughters who have been a great source of blessing to our home. My first born and her husband, Debi and Phil Zedwick, my second born and her husband, Diane and Mark Bryan, my third born and her husband, Mark and Brenda Sligar, and my fourth born and her husband, Tracey and Todd Ebeling.

They have blessed Edie and me with 13 grandchildren and one great grandson (so far). Andrew and Linda Zedwick and Justin; Shawn and David Zedwick; Kari, Jonathan and Anna Bryan; James, Amy, Christian and Michelle Sligar; Michael, Kelsey and Melissa Ebeling.

How blessed of God I have been!

Table of Contents

Foreword

One of my most memorable experiences was the day I found myself forced to climb into a small, private aircraft, with a man I hardly knew as pilot—and my awareness of his relative flying skill entirely unknown. There was nothing else to do. I had to get into the plane, which I did...with great internal discomfort.

Then, imagine my reversal of mood when, after having removed the blocks from the wheels, and having swung into his seat in the cockpit, he announced to me, "Pastor Jack, I don't know if this will make you feel any better about flying with me or not—but I have over 20,000 hours flight experience."

Whew!

We took off. And in the next half hour I learned my pilot (*Hallelujah!*) was (1) a former team member along with the legendary Chuck Yeager, part of a band of government test pilots who flew out of famed Edwards Air Force Base (where the shuttle lands today); (2) a trainer of American jet fliers for combat duty during the Korean War; and (3) a man who flew commercially as well as militarily, and had test-flown aircraft at more than twice the speed of sound!

What does that have to do with this book?

Simply this: You're about to embark with the pastoral counterpart of the pilot I just described.

Dick Iverson is a man I would trust anywhere, anytime, on any terms. He is a pastor every bit as proven in skill and reliability as my pilot that day was in aeronautical terms. You can sit back, relax, and know you're in the hands of a trustworthy practitioner.

For more than a quarter of a century I have known Pastor Iverson and observed his leadership. During the 44 years of his leadership at Portland, Oregon's famed Bible Temple (today called City Bible Church) he established a track record of growth balanced by depth, and of passionate spirituality balanced by Bible-centered solidity.

Having transferred the reins of leadership to a new generation, Dick continues in demand as a Bible teacher, pastoral conference speaker, and as a noted apostolic leader directing Ministers Fellowship International—a fellowship of more than 1000 spiritual leaders in more than 30 countries.

You may already know him, so my words are redundant for you. But someone may be reading who knows me and, taking this book in his hand may wonder, "Is this sound? Safe? Spiritually reliable?" And the answer could be (if you understand what I mean), "*He has more than 20,000 hours!*" However, sound teaching, of course, requires more than merely length of experience. It demands absolute reliability in character. And that's here too.

So that's the primary calling card I offer you as I invite you to "take flight" with Dick Iverson: Here is absolute, proven trustworthiness—absolute reliability in character and in handling God's Word of Truth.

Absolutely,

Jack W. Hayford
Chancellor-Pastor
The King's College and Seminary
The Church on the Way

Van Nuys, California
March, 2001

Preface

It has been my privilege to pastor the same church for 44 years, starting in 1951. My first 10 years were with my father as a co-pastor and then becoming senior pastor in 1961. It was not until 1965 that I fully understood my responsibility as a pastor to the congregation.

The problem I had prior to that time was that my "ministry" was more important to me than the people themselves. I failed to understand the reason I was called to pastor, which is to equip the saints for the work of the ministry (see Ephesians 4:11-12). Once I understood that my responsibility was to bring the church to maturity and release the congregation into their gifts and callings, my ministry radically changed. I had spent my first fifteen years of pastoring on a single emphasis and found it is impossible to build a mature church that way. As the scripture says, we are to give the people the whole counsel of God, and Jesus said, *"teach them to observe all things, whatsoever I have commanded you"* (Matthew 28:20).

Once I began to feed the church I watched the congregation begin to grow into maturity and that was a mark of Bible Temple (now City Bible Church). We changed from being self-centered to God-centered and we began to serve.

The messages that helped build this church are contained in this book. It was my joy to watch a congregation grow in maturity as well as numerically from the day we started with 13 people until well over 3,000 gathered Sunday after Sunday. We also established many churches out from us throughout the nation.

The strength and maturity of this congregation brought into being many peripheral ministries such as a K-12 school; a world-wide publishing company producing many teaching manuals for leaders; and Portland Bible College that has trained several thousand young people who are now all over the world, declaring the truths of God's Word. Hundreds of pastors have now linked together through a fellowship known as Ministers Fellowship International.

I give the Lord the credit and the honor for what He has done among us. The messages that you are about to read are key messages in my journey as a pastor for 44 years. May they be a blessing to you as they have been to thousands.

Dick Iverson

I wish to thank my personal secretary,

Roxy Kidder,

for the countless hours she has spent

to bring this book into reality.

Thanks, Roxy.

I also wish to thank my niece,

Cheryl Iverson,

for re-writing and editing the manuscript

along with my dear friend,

Ray Grant.

Thanks, Cheryl and Ray.

It was my joy to have my nephew,

Royce Iverson,

design the cover.

Thanks, Royce.

Releasing Truth:
The Key of David

I recently stood before a large audience and told them that in my fifty years of ministry I had given thousands of sermons. I went on to declare that if they would listen carefully to the message I was about to share that day it would be one they would never forget. I know that sounds presumptuous but I believed it to be true and say that to the reader of this chapter as well. If read carefully, we will never forget this message for it is a key that will open doors to our future. Likewise, it will shut the dark doors of unbelief, fear, and failure.

In Revelation 3, God addressed the church at Philadelphia, one of the few churches that was not heavily rebuked.

> *"And to the angel (the messenger) of the assembly (the church) in Philadelphia write: 'These are the words of the Holy One, the True One, He Who has the key of David, Who opens and no one shall shut, Who shuts and no one shall open. I know your record of works and what you are doing. See! I have set before you a door wide open, which no one is able to shut; I know that you have but little power, and yet you have kept My Word and guarded My message, and have not renounced or denied My name. Take note! I will make those of the synagogue of Satan who say they are Jews*

and are not, but lie, behold, I will make them come and bow down before your feet, and learn and acknowledge that I have loved you. Because you have guarded and kept My word of patient endurance—have held fast the lesson of My patience with the expectant endurance that I give you—I also will keep you (safe) from the hour of trial (testing) which is coming on the whole world, to try those who dwell upon the earth. I am coming quickly; hold fast what you have, so that no one may rob you and deprive you of your crown. He who overcomes (is victorious), I will make him a pillar in the sanctuary of My God." (Revelation 3:7-12, Amplified Version)

This church used a key that the Lord was pleased with—He called it the key of David. It would open doors that no one could shut and close doors that no one could open. God said the Philadelphians had received the key, because they had "...but little power" or strength. One of the requirements for experiencing the presence of God is to realize how weak we are without Him. We can have everything that looks good on the outside, but if we do not have the key of David working in our midst, we will have little power.

Isaiah 22:22-23 says, *"The key of the house of David will I lay upon his shoulder; So he shall open, and none shall shut; and he shall shut, and none shall open. And I will fasten him as a nail in a sure place."* Notice how the key of David is put upon his shoulder—God gives it to him. The same is true for us today; God will lay the key of David upon our shoulder that we may use it for His glory.

A key is something that we need to open a door. We have to have the right key as well. I have a set of keys in my pocket, but if I'm going to enter the church, it takes a certain key. Driving a car takes another, and entering a home takes another key. We cannot use just any key to open any door; the key made for that particular door is the one we need.

There is something more important in life than just a natural set of keys–it is called the key of David. With the key of David, we can be close to God, victorious, have doors open for us that no one can shut, and shut the doors that need to be shut so that we do not walk through the wrong door. The church of Philadelphia had and used this key. They did not have much strength, but because they had the right key, they were blessed people. They were able to do the work of God and guard the message that God had given them. They became very evangelistic, reached out to others, and eventually became pillars in the church. They became men and women of strength. If we are going to become pillars in the church, we need the key of David.

WHAT IS THE KEY OF DAVID?

"And it shall be, if thou wilt hearken unto all that I command thee, and wilt walk in my ways, and do that is right in my sight, to keep my statutes and my commandments, as David my servant did; that I will be with thee, and build thee a sure house, as I built for David." (1 Kings 11:38)

Responding correctly to God in every situation is the key of David. Using the key involves obedience, consistency, accountability, and having a heart after God. In James 4:8, the Bible says, *"Draw nigh to God, and he will draw nigh to you."* The key of David is that we respond to God– move closer to Him–that He, in turn, might move closer to us.

David was a man to whom God responded. The Bible includes sixty-five chapters about David alone. More is said about him than any character in the Bible other than Jesus. His name is mentioned twelve hundred times in both the Old and New Testament. Certainly his life warrants close inspection. However, what is it about the key of David that gives us open opportunities? What about the key opens doors?

Each one of us has a journey, a charge from the Lord. Each one of us has certain responsibilities that accompany that charge. The key of David will allow God to open doors of opportunity and keep them open, build for us an enduring house, both privately and corporately, and watch over us throughout our lives so that we can meet those responsibilities. We learn how to do that by studying the life of David and following his example.

Was David a super saint? No, he was not a super saint–remember he committed adultery and murder. He wasn't the greatest king, either. The Bible says Hezekiah was the greatest king. Neither was David the wisest man who ever lived. According to the scriptures, Solomon was the wisest of all men. Was it because he was sinless? No, Jesus Christ alone was sinless. So what made David so important that God says we need to have his key if success is to come our way? David knew how to correctly respond to God in every situation.

HOW DO WE RESPOND?

Our response is going to determine whether or not God opens doors. It rests on that simple equation. When the word of God comes, do we respond correctly and immediately? Or do we have to analyze it and calculate whether it is going to be effective? Our goal is to be a responder like David. By reviewing how he responded to certain situations we will learn how we are to respond to God in similar circumstances.

There are six main ingredients in responding to God the way David did:

1. David Had a Simple, Real, and Active Faith in God.

There was no religious facade with David. When the Ark of the Covenant returned to Jerusalem under David's guidance, David danced before the Ark with all his might. As he did so, his wife Michal became upset and accused him of foolishness. David's response was typical, "I am willing to act like a fool in order to show my joy in the Lord" (see 2 Samuel 6:21). David did not know how to be formal or how to put on a dignified front. But God liked David! David had no interest in what people thought about him—he was only interested in pleasing the Lord. David had a real, active faith. David said, *"I will praise thee, O Lord, with my whole heart"* (Psalm 9:1). If we will respond to God with a similar whole-hearted posture, we will begin our turning of the key of David in the doors that God wants to open for us.

2. David Was Able to Humble and Abase Himself in God's Presence.

I have an uncle who has passed on, but as a child I was very impressed with him. He was a very wealthy man. He ran for governor of Iowa and had a large real estate business. He had homes in Iowa and in Pasadena, California. He had fancy cars in both driveways. But he was also an agnostic. He had no time for God. However, as a little boy growing up, I was very impressed with Uncle Adrian. He had it made! He was "big" Uncle Adrian with big cars and a big home. Every few years my parents would visit Uncle Adrian's. I would be in awe! Uncle Adrian was about the most important person I knew.

Many years ago our church met in an old theater. One particular Sunday morning, we were having a wonderful time of worship. As I stood on the platform with my hands raised, I noticed a man enter and sit in the back row. Uncle Adrian! I could not believe it. He had never come to church before, ever, and yet here he was in the middle of this very demonstrative worship. I had my hands up, but when I saw Uncle Adrian, I found my hands coming down real fast, as I thought to myself, *I've got to get this service under control. I've got to take it away from the song leader and I've got to change the order of this service, because Uncle Adrian is here and Uncle Adrian will not understand what's going on.* When my hands were about half way down, the Lord spoke to me, "Who are you here for?" My reply was, "I'm here for you, Lord." The Lord's answer to me was, "Well, you take care of Me, and I'll take care of Uncle Adrian." Up went my hands and I forgot about Uncle Adrian.

It was one of those services where everything that can happen does! We were rejoicing, dancing and praising God. People were getting saved and healed. It was a charismatic service for sure. At the end of the service I was at the altar praying with people. I stood up and realized that Uncle Adrian was still sitting in his back row seat. I wanted to walk back and greet him, but he was a very outspoken man and would not hesitate to say what he was thinking. After such a "fanatical" service, I was sure he would have some thoughts for me.

Slowly I walked up the aisle toward him, and as I came near, I saw that his eyes were red from crying. He said, "Dick, I don't know what happened in this place, but God was here." If we take care of God, God will take care of all our Uncle Adrians. And that is what church is all about.

3. David Trusted in the Character and Integrity of God.

In my earlier ministry I was a deliverance/healing evangelist. My wife and I spent ten years traveling to many countries, praying for the sick and believing God for miracles. We witnessed many miracles during those years. Then an event took place that deeply challenged my faith.

We were expecting twins and when they were born one of them had a difficult time breathing. As a healing evangelist I prayed fervently for baby Angela in the oxygen tent, asking God to heal my child, as I had done many times before for other children.

At 4:00 AM I received a phone call from the doctor informing me that my child had died. That night was the darkest night of my life. I could not believe that death had entered into my family. God had been faithful to heal others through my ministry, but He did not heal my child. I remember telling God that I no longer wanted to be His spokesman. I symbolically shut my Bible and said, "I'm out of here. If you won't heal my child then I can't trust you any longer." I then stepped into the darkest period of my life because I lost my faith, hope, and love. For weeks I walked the floor in the middle of the night with my fist in the face of God, saying "Why, God, why?!"

One night, the Lord spoke to me through a Scripture that was out of context and had nothing to do with my child. I had turned there at His prompting in my spirit. He spoke to me out of Genesis 3:15 which says, *"And I will put enmity between thee and the woman, and between thy seed and her seed; it shall bruise thy head, and thou shalt bruise his heel."* The Lord showed me that I had been bruised with the loss of Angela, but if I would keep my faith in Him, He would let me crush the head of the enemy. Suddenly, a new breath of life came into my spirit that night and for over 40 years I have been busy crushing the head of the serpent wherever I find him.

David trusted in the character of God. In 2 Samuel 12 the Bible tells of David's response to the death of the son born to him by Bathsheba, the wife of Uriah. *"When David saw that his servants whispered, David perceived that the child was dead: therefore David said unto his servants, 'Is the child dead?' And they said, 'He is dead.'"* (verse 19).

Please notice David's response to the fact that God did not heal his son. *"Then David arose from the earth, and washed, and anointed himself, and changed his apparel, and came into the house of the Lord, and worshipped"* (verse 20).

The best place we can go when we are hurting is the presence of the Lord. When grieving, we should not grieve alone. If we will get into the presence of the Lord, we will be comforted. That was David's way and God loved it.

4. David Knew How to Handle Broken Dreams and Not Lose His Trust and Faith in God.

David wanted to be in the ministry—he wanted to build a house for the Lord. *"And it came to pass, when the king sat in his house, and the Lord had given him rest round about from all his enemies; that the king said unto Nathan the prophet, 'See now, I dwell in an house of cedar, but the ark of God dwelleth within curtains.' And Nathan said to the king, 'Go, do all that is in thine heart; for the Lord is with thee.'"* (2 Samuel 7:1-3).

One of the things that I've watched over the years is that we have a tendency to make a god out of our ministry. God does not want any gods in our lives besides Him. Nathan said to David, "Do it, the Lord is with you!" Now that should be a word from God, since Nathan is a true prophet. But then Nathan received a message from God telling him that David is not going to build a house for God. When the news came that he could not build the house, even though he had this dream and desire and had heard a prophecy, David replied, "Lord, I am in your hands." In the last part of verse 2 Samuel 7:20 David says, *"for thou, Lord GOD, knowest thy servant."*

The one thing we must always do is keep a right response to God. If He takes a dream away from us, it is probably because He is going to do something better than that dream. God is a debtor to no man. Our response will determine our future. We can get bitter and upset with God. We can say it is not right and that we have a "word" to do something. We know what God's will is, and yet doors are not opening. The key of David will open any door that God wants open and will shut any door that God wants shut. That comes from a right response to God. May our response to God be as David's, "I trust you, Lord, if you don't want me to build the house, even though I've dreamed the dream of doing it, so be it! You know your servant, you know what's best."

5. David Retained His Trust While Under the Judgment of God.

In 2 Samuel 16:6, David was walking along the road with his body-guards and mighty men around him. A man named Shimei was on the side of a hill and was cursing David and throwing stones at him. Abishai, David's servant said, *"let me go over, I pray thee, and take off his head"* (2 Samuel 16:9).

The sign of spirituality is how we treat our enemies. David's response was, *"let him curse, because the Lord hath said unto him, 'Curse David'"* (2 Samuel 16:10). David could have spoken a word and Shimei's head would have been off, rolling in the dust. But instead, David told those who were with him to leave the man alone. David's response was, "if God allows Shimei to curse me, just leave him alone. Since God has allowed it, I need it, I'll learn through it, and there will be some message to me because of it–I'll get through this."

David's response was always, "I will praise you Lord, though I have it tough and it's rough down here, I will wait patiently for You. For You will come and lift me out of the miry clay, You will set my feet on the solid rock. You will put a new song in my heart. I will wait on the Lord."

6. David Was Able to Accept a Direct Rebuke Without Excuse.

"And the Lord sent Nathan unto David. And he came unto him, and said unto him, 'There were two men in one city; the one rich, and the other poor. The rich man had exceeding many flocks and herds: But the poor man had nothing, save one little ewe lamb, which he had bought and nourished up: and it grew up together with him, and with his children; it did eat of his own meat, and drank of his own cup, and lay in his bosom, and was unto him as a daughter. And there came a traveller unto the rich man, and he spared to take of his own flock and of his

own herd, to dress for the wayfaring man that was come unto him; but took the poor man's lamb, and dressed it for the man that was come to him.' And David's anger was greatly kindled against the man; and he said to Nathan, 'As the Lord liveth, the man that hath done this thing shall surely die: and he shall restore the lamb fourfold, because he did this thing, and because he had no pity.'

And Nathan said to David, 'Thou art the man. Thus saith the Lord God of Israel, "I anointed thee king over Israel, and I delivered thee out of the hand of Saul; And I gave thee thy master's house, and thy master's wives into thy bosom, and gave thee the house of Israel and of Judah; and if that had been too little, I would moreover have given unto thee such and such things. Wherefore hast thou despised the commandment of the Lord, to do evil in his sight? Thou hast killed Uriah the Hittite with the sword, and hast taken his wife to be thy wife, and hast slain him with the sword of the children of Ammon. Now therefore the sword shall never depart from thine house; because thou hast despised me, and hast taken the wife of Uriah the Hittite to be thy wife." Thus saith the Lord, "Behold, I will raise up evil against thee out of thine own house, and I will take thy wives before thine eyes, and give them unto thy neighbour, and he shall lie with thy wives in the sight of this sun."'" (2 Samuel 12:1-11)

If ever there was an excuse needed, this was the time. David could have said to Nathan, "Now, wait a minute, Nathan, wait a minute. You've got to get something straight here. You've got to realize that she knew I was up there on that balcony. She seduced me. She disrobed herself. She knew I was up there watching."

Look again at the pronouncement—a sword in his home forever and his wives are going to be given to other men. He did not get the death sentence, but he might as well have. David could have given any number of excuses at that point and most people would have tried.

But when this pronouncement came, David simply said, *"I have sinned against the Lord"* (2 Samuel 12:13). When he needed it most, David offered absolutely no excuse. David was able to accept direct rebuke without rejecting or excusing it.

Everything rests on response. The key of David is on your shoulders. You can be like a peg that is fastened in a sure place. Even if you fall, if you respond right, there is mercy. There is forgiveness, cleansing, and restoration. David never made excuses or shifted blame. His response was "I have sinned."

How you respond to God determines your future. Your whole life is determined by your response. How do you handle broken dreams? How do you handle the dealings of God? When things do not go your way, how do you handle it? It determines whether you are going to be successful or unsuccessful.

How do you respond when God puts his finger on you? God is demanding some response from you. He does not come to beat you down or judge you. He is a father, waiting for the correct response so He can open doors for you, and give you guidance and strength.

Perhaps there is sin in your life. Perhaps it has been done secretly. David got away with it for a year or more. He thought it was hidden. But God says you cannot hide your sins and prosper. All He desires is for you to come and let Him cleanse you by a right response. *"For a just man falleth seven times, and riseth up again: but the wicked shall fall into mischief"* (Proverbs 24:16). That is how full of mercy the Lord is. But there is no mercy when there is not a right response. Instead, you will go deeper and deeper into the hole of despondency and depression, and darkness will flood over your soul. The moment you respond to the Lord, light begins to break forth and suddenly the new song comes back into your heart—and you experience God's presence again.

If you are reading this and the Holy Spirit is speaking to you, please respond. You need God's help to set you free, to deliver you, to encourage you, to lift you up. Turn your response over to God. Just say, "God, I'm going to trust you. I don't know how it's all going to turn out, but I'm going to just respond to you, and trust you. I give you the reigns of my life. I'm not going to idolize my broken dreams. I'm just going to walk with you all my life. I will be a responder."

Responding correctly to God in every situation is the key of David. Using the key involves obedience, consistency, accountability, and having a heart after God. When we respond to life like David did, God will in turn open doors of opportunity for us that no man can shut, and close doors of hardship that no man can open. The key of David will unlock your life's destiny.

CHAPTER TWO

Sustaining Truth:
Remaining Spiritually Alert

My favorite passage in the Bible is Isaiah 60. It speaks of the glory of God that is upon the house and people of God. The glory of the Lord has risen upon us!

> *"Arise, shine; for thy light is come, and the glory of the Lord is risen upon thee. For, behold, the darkness shall cover the earth, and gross darkness the people: but the Lord shall arise upon thee, and his glory shall be seen upon thee. And the Gentiles shall come to thy light, and kings to the brightness of thy rising."* (Isaiah 60:1-3)

The word "glory" simply means a manifestation of God's presence. Once in a while when we are in prayer, a worship service, or waiting on the Lord, that word comes out of our mouths: "Glory", "Glory to God!" It is a uniquely Christian term that explains the manifestation of the presence of a Holy God upon His people. Wherever God's glory is, there is a manifestation of His presence. That is why the gathering together of God's people is so important—the glory of the Lord comes and is seen upon everyone collectively. And the more glory that is evident, the more people will come to experience it. Just as a light in a dark forest attracts a variety of curious animals and birds.

The Scriptures declare that in "His presence is fullness of joy." Isaiah reminded us that when we bask in the presence of God, when we stay under His glory, awesome, practical results will occur. The results will be that people will come to know God, provision will come to our homes, our prodigal children will return.

DARKNESS AND GROSS DARKNESS

Isaiah also talked about the world being in darkness, that its people are shadowed in gross darkness. It is ironic that a world that so desperately seeks "enlightenment"—and in many cases claims to have found enlightenment—still is found to be groping in darkness. How do we battle the crime rate? Why do people crave drugs that will destroy their lives? What is the answer to divorce and broken marriages? Who can stop the shootings in high schools? Why is suicide considered a way out of the pressures of life? The world gropes in darkness for answers and solutions.

Some people turn to secular philosophies that arrive on the scene proposing some help. Psychologists formulate theories in hopes of solving the human dilemmas. Pop-psychologists try to fill in the gaps. Psychiatrists try to analyze the underlying causes of errant behavior. Each school of psychiatry has their secular solutions that differ and even contradict each other. In them, the glory of God is not evident, only more darkness.

Having given up on the confusion of the secular researchers, others have turned to enlightenment in the eastern religions, the Occult, or New Age pilgrimages. But enlightenment has also proved elusive through them.

The result of our search is a stark contrast. Isaiah talked about awesome glory and light upon the people of God—the church. He also mentions that there will be darkness in the world that will try to overcome the light we live in. Jesus confirmed this, as well as the New Testament writers. We can find scores of Scriptures that picture the church of Christ as a glorious, spotless bride for Jesus' return; a church that is full of power and glory.

CHRIST'S WARNING

Every time the return of the Lord, or Second Coming, is mentioned in the Scriptures, we will find a warning along side it. Watch out! Stay awake! Don't let the darkness snuff out your light! Don't go to sleep. *"Now it is high time to awake out of sleep: for now is our salvation nearer than when we believed."* (Romans 13:11). We are to beware, lest the darkness overtake us.

The last part of the thirteenth chapter of Mark records one of Jesus' warnings to His church. It states:

> *"But of that day and that hour knoweth no man, no, not the angels which are in heaven, neither the Son, but the Father. Take ye heed, watch and pray: for ye know not when the time is. For the Son of Man is as a man taking a far journey, who left his house, and gave authority to his servants, and to every man his work, and commanded the porter to watch. Watch ye therefore: for ye know not when the master of the house cometh, at even, or at midnight, or at the cockcrowing, or in the morning: Lest coming suddenly he find you sleeping. And what I say unto you I say unto all, Watch."* (Mark 13:32-37)

Note here that Christ is talking about His return at the Second Coming. No one knows when He will return. Through Isaiah, God warns: "Stay alert!" "Stay awake!" "Watch!" He is not talking here about physical sleep—trying to stay up all night, every night, until He comes again. He is referring to "spiritual sleep" or a spiritual stupor. He's talking about the darkness of night, cultural darkness, causing our eyes to become shut to Light—losing our alertness and growing unprepared for the return of Christ at the end of the world.

Again in Luke 21 Jesus warned his people, the church:

"Heaven and earth shall pass away: but my words shall not pass away. And take heed to yourselves, lest at any time your hearts be overcharged with surfeiting, and drunkenness, and cares of this life, and so that day come upon you unawares. For as a snare shall it come on all them that dwell on the face of the whole earth. Watch ye therefore, and pray always, that ye may be accounted worthy to escape all these things that shall come to pass, and to stand before the Son of man." (Luke 21:33-36)

The cultural world and cares of this life will weigh heavy on our shoulders, tire us out, and cause us to become sluggish and spiritually sleepy. We must watch out, or the Second Coming will be like an unexpected snare to us, just like it will be to the rest of the world in darkness.

CHOICE PASSAGES

For any major theological or practical spiritual subject, there is usually one particular chapter or passage that speaks directly to that subject. For instance, it if wanted a lofty passage about "love" we would quickly turn to 1 Corinthians 13, "the love chapter." If we wanted to know about the Kingdom of God we would turn to Matthew 13. And if we desired to understand the resurrection we would look at 1 Corinthians 15. Whole sections of scriptures are given to us to help us understand these major doctrines in the Bible.

Jesus wanted his church to stay alert, not go to sleep. So He gave us a major passage of scripture which, if we listen to, will keep us from going to sleep. It will keep us from becoming an apostate.

One day years ago I was meditating and asking myself what things were keeping our church alive, well, and awake. My wife and I had started as senior pastors in 1961 and we had experienced quite a few cultural transitions. The Vietnam War with all its turmoil, drugs, and protests. The hippie revolution. A president assassinated. The transition in music and movies; the rise in pornography; the sexual revolution. But our church remained stable during those times. We had steady growth—in fact, we had planted several churches then.

I began to list all those things I thought were necessary to maintain that stability and growth. I put down important principles I thought should be present in a church that does not go to sleep. As I was writing these down, I suddenly discovered that God had put an entire chapter in the Bible that covered this list. The ingredients of a strong church that was aware and alert were already recorded.

CHECK LIST

First Thessalonians 5 contains most of those necessary ingredients that will keep a church from going to sleep. All of these ingredients are necessary. If we take one out, or let another become insignificant, we are risking the spiritual health of our church. Our church will become vulnerable. It will be open to sudden attack from unexpected sources because we were not alert.

If we take heed to all of these admonitions listed by the Apostle Paul, our churches will not be affected by the darkness around them. The stock market can go up or down. The economy can waver. Crime can increase and global warming can continue. Through it all, the church will keep growing.

Let me quote the entire passage that I found to contain the necessary ingredients for helping a church stay alert spiritually:

"But of the times and the seasons, brethren, ye have no need that I write unto you. For yourselves know perfectly that the day of the Lord so cometh as a thief in the night. For when they shall say, 'Peace and safety;' then sudden destruction cometh upon them, as travail upon a woman with child; and they shall not escape. But ye, brethren, are not in darkness, that that day should overtake you as a thief. Ye are all the children of light, and the children of the day: we are not of the night, nor of darkness.

"Therefore let us not sleep, as do others; but let us watch and be sober. For they that sleep sleep in the night; and they that be drunken are drunken in the night. But let us, who are of the day, be sober, putting on the breastplate of faith and love; and for an helmet, the hope of salvation. For God hath not appointed us to wrath, but to obtain salvation by our Lord Jesus Christ, Who died for us, that, whether we wake or sleep, we should live together with him. Wherefore comfort yourselves together, and edify one another, even as also ye do. And we beseech you, brethren, to know them which labour among you, and are over you in the Lord, and admonish you; and to esteem them very highly in love for their work's sake. And be at peace among yourselves. Now we exhort you, brethren, warn them that are unruly, comfort the feebleminded, support the weak, be patient toward all men. See that none render evil for evil unto any man; but ever follow that which is good, both among yourselves, and to all men. Rejoice evermore. Pray without ceasing. In every thing give thanks: for this is the will of God in Christ Jesus concerning you. Quench not the Spirit. Despise not prophesyings. Prove all things; hold fast that which is good. Abstain from all appearance of evil. And the very God of

peace sanctify you wholly; and I pray God your whole spirit and soul and body be preserved blameless unto the coming of our Lord Jesus Christ. Faithful is he that calleth you, who also will do it." (1 Thessalonians 5:1-24)

God has not left us to wonder about how to keep alert or awake when darkness bids us sleep. He inspired Paul to write to the church at Thessalonica, and to us, to show us how we can stay aware of the times in which we live.

There are many churches that start out alive and well, but over the course of time become institutionalized; they lose their appreciation for the vision given to them in the beginning and just die out. I've been in churches with beautiful facilities that are only a memorial to the past, a tombstone commemorating a past day.

We never want that to happen. We do not want to say, "I remember the good old days," because the church is no longer very good. No, the good days are to be happening right now. There are certain requirements we have to meet in order for that to take place.

A REAL ENEMY

The enemy, our adversary the Devil, wants to put us to sleep. He would like to bring our churches into apostasy. Our culture, the world system, is designed to spiritually drain us. The enemy is at war with the church. If the book of Revelation reveals anything, it shows that the Devil is against the church militantly. He does not like the kingdom of God. He desperately tries to "wear out the saints." Take away our spiritual strength. Sap the daylight out of us. "Wear out" means to exhaust someone. When we are exhausted, we become tired. We will become weak. And soon we are asleep.

But God gave this entire passage of 1 Thessalonians 5 that tells us exactly what it will take to keep our churches on the cutting edge of what God is doing until Jesus comes back. I believe the church was designed to be eternal. I know there are a lot of churches that have had a lifetime of ten or twenty years and they fade away and become nonexistent. But that is not God's will. The church is not to pass away, but to pass on to the next generation strong and healthy, fulfilling the will of God in the earth and showing forth God's glory to bring honor to His name.

THE LIST

The darker the culture around us becomes, the greater our need for spiritual alertness. When gross darkness envelops a society, the greater the need for the church to manifest the glorious light of the Gospel. The church must not lower its standards.

1. Cultural Awareness

"But of the times and the seasons, brethren, ye have no need that I write unto you. For yourselves know perfectly that the day of the Lord so cometh as a thief in the night. For when they shall say, 'Peace and safety;' then sudden destruction cometh upon them, as travail upon a woman with child; and they shall not escape." (1 Thessalonians 5:1-3)

The church must be alert to its cultural environment. We must know "the times and seasons." We are told in 1 Chronicles 12:32 that the tribe of Issachar were men who had *"understanding of the times, to know what Israel ought to do."* They were alert; and so we ought to be alert, as we wait for the coming of the Lord.

The world does not understand its purpose in history, nor are they aware of the tremendous role it will play in the return of Jesus. To the Ephesians, Paul wrote that the *". . .Gentiles walk, in the vanity of their mind, having the understanding darkened, being alienated from the life of God through the ignorance that is in them, because of the blindness of their heart"* (Ephesians 4:17-18). Sin and spiritual gross darkness blinds their minds.

The same was true of the Jewish elders at the first coming of Christ. The last time Jesus entered Jerusalem before His crucifixion, He wept and said, *"If you had known, even you, especially in this your day, the things that make for your peace! But now they are hidden from your eyes. . . because you did not know the time of your visitation."* (Luke 19:42,44). They were not awake to the very presence of God in their midst. And it had serious consequences to them as they crucified God.

Both Jew and Gentile, Paul wrote, are lacking in alertness. *"There is none that understandeth, there is none that seeketh after God. They are all gone out of the way. . ."* (Romans 3:11-12). It is the same in our world today. Men need to start seeking God to understand the times. Like Daniel of old, we all need to *"set thine heart to understand, and to chasten thyself before thy God. . ."* (Daniel 10:12) by seeking God and getting into His Word. The psalmist declared, *"through thy precepts I get understanding."* (Psalm 119:104). John also wrote, *"And we know that the Son of God is come, and hath given us an understanding. . ."* (1 John 5:20).

Destruction comes upon those who lack understanding of the time they are living in. Just as Jerusalem was conquered and destroyed, so also those who live worldly lives will be caught in sudden destruction at the second coming of Christ. Here in Thessalonians it declares that God's intention for the church is to be awake, and that it will not be overtaken if it stays that way. If it recognizes the seductive nature of the worldly church and remains pure, maintains its separateness and holiness, and recognizes it is at war with its culture, the church will overcome!

2. Biblical Identity

"Ye are all the children of light, and the children of the day: we are not of the night, nor of darkness. Therefore let us not sleep, as do others; but let us watch and be sober. For they that sleep sleep in the night; and they that be drunken are drunken in the night."
(1 Thessalonians 5:5-7)

We are the children of light! We can be spiritually alert by knowing who we are in Christ Jesus. We are children of God, children of light, sons of the Most High! We need to recognize who we all are in Christ! Redeemed, blood-bought, sanctified, freed, cleansed, enlightened, Spirit-filled, anointed sons and daughters of almighty God!

If we do not understand who we are in Christ, Satan will fill us with doubts, condemnation, and depression. He will beat us down at every turn. He is the accuser of the brethren. He will let us know if we do not pray enough or read the Bible enough. After a while we are just glad they even let us come through the front door of the church any more. *I'm such a weak person,* we think. But that is the Devil talking. Pretty soon, we are all blinded to the potential we have in Christ. We are so depressed that we just want to cower in a corner and go to sleep.

But Paul here is reminding us of our Biblical identity. He is reminding us of who we are: children of Light and sons of God. Because He knows that if we know who we are, we will start acting like it. He knows that knowledge will help us stay alert and awake. We will not succumb to behaving like the world, because we are of God and all He stands for: peace, purity, soberness, cleanliness, etc. We will uphold his standards of conduct, so that at the Second Coming, we can hear Jesus say, "Well done, my good and faithful servants." At that time we will not be caught blinded by sin and wallowing in it.

The church must be proud of who they are, and of who Jesus is! There is something about the Bible and the Christian life that is very positive! We will never find words like, "you can do some things through Christ who strengthens you." Or, "you're more than conquerors some of the time." "If God is for you most of the time, who can be against you?" We do not find any of that kind of language. It is always, "I am for you." The Lord is for us! The Lord is our strength. We can do all things through Christ! Greater is He that is in us that he that is in the world.

God is greater than our problems. God is bigger than our weaknesses. God is more powerful than the Devil. That is the truth that keeps us all alert so that we do not go to sleep. The world uses positive thinking and believes that mental exercise will be enough. They see the value in being positive and having a positive identity. But the Bible tells us we are to speak words of faith about ourselves in Christ. If we do not want to go to sleep, then we say, "The scriptures confirm that 'I am complete in Him.' I may not feel like it, I may not even look like it, but I believe it! The Lord is my righteousness." These truths are things that keep us alive and well.

3. Three Motivating Forces

"But let us, who are of the day, be sober, putting on the breastplate of faith and love; and for an helmet, the hope of salvation."
(1 Thessalonians 5:8)

For a soldier to be ready and alert he must be fully armored. When he is, he will be ready at a moment's notice to move out against his foe. The Christian must also be spiritually equipped in order to remain alert. And what is this armor? It is faith, hope, and love.

When we put these on—that is, when we equip our minds and hearts with them—the church is motivated to stay awake. Just as a helmet provides protection for the head, so hope provides mental protection. Without hope, a person just does not feel like going on in life. Hopelessness saps energy and motivation for living. And when we are spiritually tired we fall asleep. But the Bible says that we are to hope in God! *"Why art though cast down, O my soul? And why art thou disquieted in me? Hope thou in God!"* (Psalm 42:5). Peter confirms this by saying, *"Wherefore gird up the loins of your mind, be sober, and hope to the end for the grace that is to be brought unto you at the revelation of Jesus Christ!"* (1 Peter 1:13).

It is the same with faith. If there is a loss of faith, we become aimless wanderers. We have to believe in something to give life meaning. Doubt and skepticism open wide the door to failure and despair. The goal of Satan is to cause the people of God to lose faith in the future, in the prophetic word, in the church, and even in God. "I've waited so long for these prophecies to be fulfilled. I've tried to believe for so long, but...." Soon despair sets in and we return to our worldly ways. We need to keep our faith. The apostle John underscores this, *"For whatsoever is born of God overcometh the world: and this is the victory that overcometh the world, even our faith"* (1 John 5:4).

Love must be in our hearts as well. Love is expressed in relationships. Because of that, Satan wants to break up relationships in the church, starting with God. Many people turn against God because of some disappointment in life. They were planning something and it did not turn out the way they thought it would. They lost a job. A close family member died of sickness. They ask, "Why God?" and turn against Him.

Relationships within the church can also become strained. We disappoint others, and others disappoint us. We get offended by leaders, or we offend the leaders. The Bible states that offenses will occur. But love keeps relationships alive! In spite of the daily little bumps in the road, the set-backs and disappointments, love will overcome. Love thinks the best, even in bad circumstances. Sometimes we have to keep loving even though it is not reciprocal. Sometimes we have to love God when He does not feel very close. But love will sustain us through those hard times. It will keep us protected from the snare of the Devil.

Faith, hope, and love—we must never lose these. We will never have all the answers as we go through life, but in the meantime, until Jesus comes back, we must keep believing, hoping, and showing love.

4. Intimate Relationship with God

"For God hath not appointed us to wrath, but to obtain salvation by our Lord Jesus Christ, Who died for us, that, whether we wake or sleep, we should live together with him." (1 Thessalonians 5:9-10)

It is most important to keep our spiritual momentum by maintaining the intimate relationship with our Savior, Jesus Christ. It does not matter whether we are living on this earthly planet or existing in the next life in heaven, we live together with Him.

"Live together" brings to mind the marriage concept. Two people who are wed in holy matrimony live together. They flow through life together. They work at marriage together. They raise children together. Their goals and aspirations are fulfilled together.

Revelation 19:7 says, *"His wife has made herself ready."* Corporately, the church has a relationship with the Lord that we must maintain. This is the essence of the church. We are here to form a habitation for God's spirit. God wants to dwell in the midst of His people and we must maintain that intimacy with the Lord Jesus. When we do, we will remain spiritually awake.

5. The Body of Christ

"Wherefore comfort yourselves together, and edify one another, even as also ye do." (1 Thessalonians 5:11)

There is something about the corporate gathering that cannot be reproduced when alone. We will not find it in home meetings. There is something about the time when the whole church comes together that cannot be surpassed. That something is the dynamic flow of the Spirit of God reverberating through each member and ministering to each one. One member is a "hand," one is "foot," another is an "ear," and they minister in their function to the whole body. The dynamic cannot be experienced any other way.

If there was anything that changed my life for the better, it was when God helped me to understand the church. I was an evangelist then and thought the church was there to help support my great evangelistic ministry. But I was made to realize that I am not there to be supported by the church, but to support them and their individual ministries to the whole body. God finally helped me to see that the leadership ministry is there to help each member rise up unto the work of ministering to each other, just like the eye, ear, and foot all minister and serve the whole body (see Ephesians 4:11-13). The body is not just a crowd of people, not an audience, but individual people who need each other.

If we are not going to be caught napping at the Second Coming, we have to be sure we have a correct understanding of our relationship to each person in the church. It does not mean we agree with everything each person does, but we exercise patience and longsuffering and respect to each other, as unto Christ.

6. Spiritual Leadership

"And we beseech you, brethren, to know them which labour among you, and are over you in the Lord, and admonish you; and to esteem them very highly in love for their work's sake. And be at peace among yourselves." (1 Thessalonians 5:12-13)

No church can be alert without respect and love for its leadership. It cannot make it through an adverse society and wicked culture without orderly administration. Leadership must be respected if the church is to remain spiritually alert.

While we do recognize the "priesthood of all believers" it does not mean total independence or separation from the body. Just as we need the body of Christ to work together for spiritual alertness, so also we need good relationships with church leadership. We are not to honor them to the point of deity, nor are we to write them off as useless. Instead, we are to work with them in establishing the church.

The Apostle Peter affirmed Paul's admonition: *"Elders. . .shepherd the flock of God . . . you younger people, submit yourselves to your elders. Yes, all of you be submissive to one another, and be clothed with humility"* (1 Peter 5:1-8). And then Peter warns about the roaring lion who wants to devour us by telling us to *"Be sober, be vigilant"* (1 Peter 5:8).

The writer of the book of Hebrews also repeated this counsel. *"Remember those who have the rule over you. . . obey those who rule over you. . . Greet all those who rule over you."* (Hebrews 13:7,17,24). When we do that, our spiritual alertness will remain.

7. Church Discipline

"Now we exhort you, brethren, warn them that are unruly, comfort the feebleminded, support the weak, be patient toward all men. See that none render evil for evil unto any man; but ever follow that which is good, both among yourselves, and to all men" (1 Thessalonians 5:14-15)

We must appreciate loving discipline in the house of God. We will never have a strong, productive church without discipline. Just like we will never have a good home if there is no discipline of the children in the home. This is how we raise a natural family, and this is how we maintain purity and holiness in the church.

Some members are head-strong and need consistent discipline. Others only need instruction and patience. Some are unruly and need correction; others are merely misguided and need only guidance. But we are warned in verse 15 that our discipline is not for vengeance. It is not to destroy the erring brother. In other letters, Paul states that the main purpose of discipline is restoration (see Galatians 6:1-8). Discipline should be highly valued. It keeps the church in good working order and alert for Christ's coming.

8. Joy of the Lord

"Rejoice evermore!" (1 Thessalonians 5:16)

We must never lose the joy of the Lord! The sign of an apostate, dead church is silence and somberness. Some people complain, "I see fanatics praising God, waving their arms, clapping their hands. I even see them jumping up and down at times! Can't they keep silence in the house of the Lord?"

The apostate church is marked by silence because the Devil does not want joy in the house of the Lord. If he can drain us of our joy, he can shut off our witness, causing us to lose our influence in the world. The best witnesses and soul winners are often brand new converts because of their unbridled enthusiasm. That is, until someone boxes them in, constrains them, and drains them of their joy.

When I was a little kid we would open our presents on Christmas morning. It made Christmas Eve the longest night of the year. We were required to stay in bed until 6:00 AM. I would take one of those ticking clocks and put it right under my pillow. I would try to sleep with it there. It would seem that I slept for an hour or two and I would open my eyes and look at the clock. Only ten minutes had passed! It was the same all night long. Why? Because I was excited about what was going to happen in the morning.

We cannot put a person to sleep if he is excited. Likewise, we can never lose the joy of the Lord. It is the mark of a church that is alive and well, not sleeping. A joyous church is one that is alive, alert and awake.

9. Communion with God

"Pray without ceasing." (1 Thessalonians 5:17)

An alert church must have an ongoing, open line of communication with God. Luke related the story of Jesus praying in the Garden of Gethsemane and told of an angel coming to Him and "strengthening" Him (see Luke 22:43-46). Then Jesus went to His disciples and found them sleeping.

Jesus nudged them, and said unto them, *"Why sleep ye? Rise and pray, lest ye enter into temptation."* They were missing out. If they had been praying, in spite of their exhaustion, the angel would strengthen them too! They did not realize they needed strength for the days ahead.

The easiest way for a church to go to sleep is to have it stop its prayer life. If we quit scheduling the prayer meetings of the church, move on to cultural issues and programs only, its life and vitality will soon be drained dry. If we keep an ongoing prayer vigil, the church will be alive and energetic. When our prayers resound in the corridors of heaven we stay on the cutting edge of life. Our church will make a difference in the history of mankind.

10. A Grateful Spirit

"In every thing give thanks: for this is the will of God in Christ Jesus concerning you." (1 Thessalonians 5:18)

If we maintain a grateful spirit, we will not fall spiritually asleep. In everything, we are to give thanks! It is God's will for us. Instead of mumbling, grumbling, and complaining, we need to say, "Thank you, God, for my salvation, my family, my church, my Bible. Thank you for the privilege of knowing You. Thank you for peace of mind."

We need to not only thank Him for the blessings, but also for the adversity of life. *"Blessed are you when they revile and persecute you, and say all kinds of evil against you falsely for My sake. Rejoice and be exceedingly glad, for great is your reward in heaven,"* Jesus said in Matthew 5:11-12. This grateful attitude will keep us from being discouraged and dragged down spiritually. The Devil cannot put a person to sleep who is vibrating with the appreciation and anticipation of a grateful spirit. *"Rejoice in the Lord always. Again, I will say rejoice!"* (Philippians 4:4).

11. Prophetic Voice

"Quench not the Spirit. Despise not prophesyings. Prove all things; hold fast that which is good." (1 Thessalonians 5:19-21)

One of the most exciting things about the coming together of the people of God is the manifestation of God in their midst. God has not left us orphans. He is not a "deist" type of God who sits in the heavens aloof. He continues to show His care for His church by continuing to speak to His people. What would we think of a parent who gave birth to children but never talked to them or encouraged them? We would most likely think about turning them in for child abuse.

Today, many churches do not believe in prophecy. Many believe God quit speaking two thousand years ago. It just does not fit into their theology, or their dispensational scheme of things. But God has set prophets in the church, just as he put pastors and teachers into leadership. Have pastors and teachers been eliminated? No. Neither have prophets. (See Ephesians 4:11-13.) They are all in the body to minister to it.

Therefore, as the Holy Spirit says: "Today, if you will hear His voice, Do not harden your hearts as in the rebellion. . . " (Hebrews 3:7-8 NKJV). The writer of the book of Hebrews quoted the psalmist in the Old Testament. Back then, God was a "today" God—He spoke to their immediate need. In New Testament times, God spoke directly through His Son, and through the prophets in the church (see Hebrews 1:2; Acts

3:33, 11:28). The writer of Hebrews said there were still "todays" in which God speaks (3:13). We are to listen "today." God is still speaking to His church.

In order to hear from God, we have to "have ears to hear," for Revelation repeatedly stated *"He that hath an ear, let him hear what the Spirit saith unto the churches"* (2:7, 11, 17, 29, etc.). Many churches are missing out on blessings because they do not think the Spirit will talk to them any more. It was the Spirit's words to the seven churches in Revelation that was keeping them alert and pure. Today is no different. If we will have ears to hear what the Spirit is saying to us, we will remain spiritually alert.

12. Avoidance of Sin

"Abstain from all appearance of evil." (1 Thessalonians 5:22)

There is so much cultural compromise in Christian circles today. If the world does it, some in the church seem to think the church should be doing it as well. It seems the church just follows after the fashions, styles, and practices of the world. The way the world talks, dresses, and performs becomes so commonplace after time that the church just assimilates that into the church talk, dress, and conduct. The church slowly, gradually lowers its standards and thus loses its distinctiveness form the world. It takes on the "form" of the world, or as the Apostle Paul put it, is *"conformed to this world"* (Romans 12:2).

Paul warns if we are to remain alert and awake, we must abstain from all forms of evil. We are not to compromise or see how close we can get to the fire without getting burned. If someone abstains from alcohol, it means no alcohol whatsoever. He does not sip a little here, sip a little there. We are to abstain from worldly ways.

There is a story I heard as a young person about the Old West and its stagecoach drivers. They were an elite class of men, selected for their skill and daring. They had to transport Wells Fargo passengers and valuables over the majestic Rocky Mountains, a very dangerous job.

One day there was a sign posted: "Wanted: Stage Coach Drivers for Wells Fargo." Many cowboys lined up for the interview. As they came in, they were asked one question: "If you were out on a mountain road, and there was a cliff on one side, and you were driving this stagecoach, how close could you come to the edge and still have it under control?"

One cowboy said, "I can come within a foot and still have it under control!" Another bragged, "I could come within six inches and still have those horses under control." One by one they gave their answer until they finally came to one wise cowboy.

When asked the question, he replied, "Well, I don't look at it quite the way the others do. I never see how close to the edge I can come. I always try to get as far away from the edge as I can!" "You've got the job!" was the company's response. And that is the message here. We are to shun evil—every part of it. If we do, its seduction or enticements will not lull us. We will not fall asleep.

God is faithful to help us remain spiritually awake. If we do these twelve things, we will maintain our ability to walk uprightly before the Lord. As Paul puts it, *"And the very God of peace sanctify you wholly; and I pray God your whole spirit and soul and body be preserved blameless unto the coming of our Lord Jesus Christ. Faithful is he that calleth you, who also will do it"* (1 Thessalonians 5:23-24).

Sanctifying Truth:
Drawing Lines

Drawing lines to guide our lives in modern society is not easy. In the Bible, God gives us principles to live by that shine light on our daily walk. If we are following Christ, the lines we draw must be in harmony with these principles and these lines will govern our daily activities. These three levels of understanding are not original with me. However, I would like to enlarge upon them in greater application in this chapter. There are three types of guidelines which affect our lives:

1. Biblical Mandates

Clear commands from the Bible separate sinful behavior from righteous behavior in specific circumstances. God draws these lines which prohibit certain activities and require certain others. These lines are absolute. They are not up for debate. They require the obedience of all Christians in every nation and culture under heaven.

2. Personal Convictions

God deals sovereignly with each believer to establish personal disciplines in individual lives. These personal codes of conduct prepare believers for unique, God-ordained tasks that differ from person to person. Only you must follow personal disciplines and convictions God has given you. Mistaking personal convictions with biblical mandates leads to many relational conflicts among believers.

3. Community Standards

Desirable behavior within groups is defined by community. Group leaders set the standards for the group's conduct. From group to group, business to business and from church to church, community standards vary, but their purpose is to keep the group in smooth, working order. Standards establish a foundation for relationships between community members and enable a community to govern itself.

VARIETY AND CONTROVERSY

A knock on my motel room door announced the arrival of the six elders. They were from a strong "holiness" church. I was in their city at their invitation speaking at a series of evangelistic meetings in their church. They came into the room looking very sober.

"We would like to talk with you," said one of the elders.

"Fine," I answered as I welcomed them. They sat down. I could tell something was seriously troubling them.

"We believe in holiness," the spokesman for the group said. "In our church we believe there are certain things we should do and certain things we should never do."

I could see I had offended them, but I had no idea what I had done. I tried to be agreeable.

"We do not believe in wearing jewelry," the spokesman finally said as they all stared at my ring.

I was wearing a little stainless steel ring I had made while in high school. "You mean this ring?" I asked as I pointed to my finger.

"Yes," they answered. "We do no believe anyone, especially a minister, would wear jewelry if he is serious about true holiness before God."

At this point I had two choices:

Choice A:

I could say, "Bless God, if your faith is so weak that a little piece of metal is going to keep you from entering in today, then...."

Choice B:

As I remove the ring I could say, "I am very sorry. Please forgive me. I would never want to offend you."

Variety may be the spice of life but in the church it leads to conflict. It causes PROBLEMS! Christian brothers and sisters with different opinions, preferences, and personal convictions speak their views and often impose those views on other believers.

"I would never do what Bob does," says one believer. "I think it is sin and Bob should not do it either!"

Christians hold a wide range of views on music, movies, dress, social drinking, gambling, dancing, money, child discipline, and education. Everyone in the church has a different opinion and some opinions are quite rigid. Left unchecked, controversy will kill unity in the church and will lead to severe conflict.

"For, brethren, ye have been called unto liberty; only use not liberty for an occasion to the flesh, but by love serve one another. For all the law is fulfilled in one word, even in this; thou shalt love thy neighbour as thyself. But if ye bite and devour one another, take heed that ye be not consumed one of another." (Galatians 5:13-15)

Sad to say, I have seen people who have been torn up because of a difference with another brother or sister. I have seen friendships dissolve and, on a larger scale, entire churches divide. However, the differences causing these problems are usually differences in preference or opinion in areas where the Bible leaves room for liberty and variety. Seldom have I seen a difference over the clear commands of the Word of God.

I am constantly amazed that believers in the one God who have one Bible can have so many areas of difference. Yet the evidence seen in churches all over the world suggests that God can reap a tremendous harvest and send His life to flow through believers who have great differences and may even sit together in the same assembly. People can have many differences in personal interpretation, but if they maintain an attitude of unity God can work mightily through them.

It is exciting to see the body of Christ in unity, because in unity is power. In unity is life. In unity we receive blessing. The reverse is true when the church is not unified. We have no life, no blessing, and no power. We have strife, division, and death.

CLEAR COMMANDS

We should never argue over the clear commands of the Word of God. If we love Him, we will keep His commands. We trust and obey His clear Word because that is what it means to be a believer. Clear, unmistakable, absolute, nonnegotiable mandates cannot be questioned. God draws these lines. He draws them around specific activities and does not allow variation from person to person or between cultures.

Specific biblical mandates prohibit Christians from idol worship, sexual immorality, murder, stealing, lying, drunkenness, and coveting things that belong to another person, to name a few. Other biblical mandates require diligence in employment, wholesome speech, respect for authority, a willingness to serve others, and wise handling of money. The Word of God also clearly encourages godly attitudes like dependability, patience, humility, courage, and kindness.

God drew these lines for our good. Blessings come to us as from life within the borders of the path marked for us by God.

GRAY AREAS

Differences between Christians most often arise over things not clearly labeled good or bad in the Bible. Some activities are neither encouraged nor specifically prohibited in the Bible. When Scripture does not directly judge an activity or a behavior, we have to allow room for variety among God's people. God has delegated to us the privilege of drawing these lines in our own spheres of influence. Following principles of the Word of God, individuals draw lines to establish personal convictions and groups initiate community standards for self-government.

With the privilege of establishing a code of conduct comes the responsibility to discern the lines of demarcation between clear biblical mandates, community standards, and personal convictions. All three govern our lives daily. We need to see where the lines are and what happens when they overlap or collide with other believers.

WHERE LINES CROSS

Going back to the day I was confronted by the elders about wearing jewelry, we had a difference. I had liberty to wear my ring but they considered it sin. Without a biblical mandate for or against jewelry, I took off my ring and apologized for the offense. When differences like this take place, a collision may occur with someone saying, "We should not do it that way. I do not agree. I do not like what that person is doing."

Through the years I have pastored, I have known people to enjoy certain "liberties" which make me very uncomfortable. How much television should a Christian watch? How about movies, dancing, or drinking? Is there a line between what is acceptable and what is not? What guides us in relation to these important issues?

We all tend to approach these questions with personal preferences and opinions. Not all of us have had the same training. Not all come from the same cultural background or from the same country. God brings people into the church from a great variety of different backgrounds with as many different perspectives. Can we really worship and work together without our attention being drawn to those areas in which we differ? As long as we always take the approach that we prefer others before ourselves, I think we can.

God knows all about man. He knows our attraction to sin, selfishness, and pride. He is not surprised by different concepts and practices threatening the unity of His church. The Holy Spirit prompted the apostle Paul to write the fourteenth chapter of Romans to address the so-called "gray" areas of Christian behavior. The instruction is balanced as God's word always is. It is clear and precise without being rigid. It draws boundary lines for Christian behavior, yet allows for variety and creativity within the boundaries. It points us down the narrow way which leads to abundant life.

"Him that is weak in the faith receive ye, but not to doubtful disputations. For one believeth that he may eat all things: another, who is weak, eateth herbs. Let not him that eateth despise him that eateth not; and let not him which eateth not judge him that eateth: for God hath received him. Who art thou that judgest another man's servant? To his own master he standeth or falleth. Yea, he shall be holden up: for God is able to make him stand. One man esteemeth one day above another: another esteemeth every day alike. Let every man be fully persuaded in his own mind. He that regardeth the day, regardeth it unto the Lord; and

he that regardeth not the day, to the Lord he doth not regard it. He that eateth, eateth to the Lord, for he giveth God thanks; and he that eateth not, to the Lord he eateth not, and giveth God thanks. For none of us liveth to himself, and no man dieth to himself. For whether we live, we live unto the Lord; and whether we die, we die unto the Lord: whether we live therefore, or die, we are the Lord's. For to this end Christ both died, and rose, and revived, that he might be Lord both of the dead and living. But why dost thou judge thy brother? Or why dost thou set at nought thy brother? For we shall all stand before the judgment seat of Christ. For it is written, 'As I live, saith the Lord, every knee shall bow to me, and every tongue shall confess to God.' So then every one of us shall give account of himself to God. Let us not therefore judge one another any more: but judge this rather, that no man put a stumblingblock or an occasion to fall in his brother's way. I know, and am persuaded by the Lord Jesus, that there is nothing unclean of itself: but to him that esteemeth any thing to be unclean, to him it is unclean. But if thy brother be grieved with thy meat, now walkest thou not charitably. Destroy not him with thy meat, for whom Christ died. Let not then your good be evil spoken of: For the kingdom of God is not meat and drink; but righteousness, and peace, and joy in the Holy Ghost. For he that in these things serveth Christ is acceptable to God, and approved of men. Let us therefore follow after the things which make for peace, and things wherewith one may edify another. For meat destroy not the work of God. All things indeed are pure; but it is evil for that man who eateth with offence. It is good neither to eat flesh, nor to drink wine, nor any thing whereby thy brother stumbleth, or is offended, or is made weak. Hast thou faith? Have it to thyself before God. Happy is he that condemneth not himself in that thing which he alloweth. And he that doubteth is damned if he eat, because he eateth not of faith: for whatsoever is not of faith is sin." (Romans 14:1-23)

BIBLICAL MANDATES

"My words shall not pass away." (Matthew 24:35)

The Word of God will never pass away. It is sure, reliable, and unchangeable because God Himself is sure, reliable, and unchangeable. God cannot lie (see Titus 1:2). *"God is not a man, that he should lie; neither the son of man, that he should repent [change His mind]"* (Numbers 23:19). *"For I am the Lord, I change not"* (Malachi 3:6).

The Bible is the only consistent standard available to mankind. It is God's Law. Through the Bible, God draws lines for us to follow and by which to live. The Word of God is *"a lamp unto my feet, and a light unto my path"* (Psalm 119:105). The Bible is like an operation or owner's manual for us, telling you and me how to live.

God gave us His Word for our good. Sometimes we do not understand God's laws and must obey them by faith, but we know everything God requires of us is for our good. He is interested in helping us (see Jeremiah 29:11).

Biblical mandates are absolutes. They are not up for debate. They do not change. They draw lines between sin and righteousness in specific circumstances. God leaves no room for different opinions or preferences where He gives clear commands.

Biblical mandates require our obedience. They apply to every man, woman, and child in the world. It does not matter into which family or culture we were born. *"the Lord thy God hath commanded thee to do these statutes and judgments... with all thine heart, and with all thy soul"* (Deuteronomy 26:16). Jesus said, *"If ye love me, keep my commandments"* (John 14:15).

Obeying biblical mandates is not the thankless task some people pretend it to be. Rewards await the obedient and help believers keep good attitudes when they face difficulties. In the same way, the joy set before Christ helped Him endure the cross (see Hebrews 12:2).

Rewards for obedience include, but are not limited to:

1. **Being God's "Special Treasure"** (see Exodus 19:5).
2. **Long Life** (see 1 Kings 3:14).
3. **Things Working out Well** (see Deuteronomy 5:16).
4. **The Blessing of God** (see Luke 11:28).
5. **Strength and Stability** (see Luke 6:47-48).
6. **A Crown of Life** (see Revelation 2:10).
7. **Entry to the Eternal City** (see Revelation 22:14).

IDENTIFYING BIBLICAL MANDATES

Christ's words confirm biblical mandates for today. Believers are to submit themselves to all of Christ's commands included in the new covenant or New Testament. God deals with man based on covenant. The new covenant retains much of what is in the Old Testament teachings. Certain ceremonial duties and regulations from Old Testament covenants were nailed to the Cross (see Colossians 2:14). They were fulfilled in Christ (see Luke 24:44) and abolished (see Ephesians 2:15). We have no reason or desire to go back and resurrect Judaism and the Mosaic Covenant. However, according to hermeneutical principles, any Old Testament teaching endorsed in the New Testament by Jesus remains in effect today. Therefore, one must look for Jesus' endorsement to identify New Testament biblical mandates in order to distinguish them from personal convictions and community standards.

For example, adultery is condemned in both the Old and New Testaments. This is not an issue that is up for debate. We cannot pick and choose our own preference in this matter. God made it very, very clear. *Thou shalt not commit adultery"* (Exodus 20:14). Jesus reaffirmed the mandate against adultery (see Matthew 19:17-18). Any premarital or extramarital sexual relationship (including mental adultery and pornography) by definition is either adultery or fornication. Outside the bond of marriage, sex is immoral and destructive. The evidence is all around us. Adultery and fornication tear down people spiritually, mentally, physically, and socially. You and I cannot argue with this mandate. It is an absolute law of God established in the days of Moses and confirmed by Christ.

The Bible also places the following activities outside the lines of acceptable behavior for God's people:

1. **Idolatry** (see Exodus 20:4; 1 Corinthians 6:9)
2. **Blaspheming** (see Exodus 20:7; Colossians 3:8)
3. **Murder** (see Exodus 20:13; Matthew 19:17-18)
4. **Stealing** (see Exodus 20:15; Matthew 19:17-18)
5. **Lying** (see Exodus 20:16; Matthew 19:17-18)
6. **Envy and Jealousy** (see Exodus 20:17; Galatians 5:21)
7. **Drunkenness** (see Proverbs 23;20-21; Ephesians 5:18)
8. **Homosexuality** (see Leviticus 18:22; 20:13; 1 Timothy 1:10)

DOCTRINAL TRUTH

Doctrinal truths like the deity of Christ and justification by faith stand solidly on absolute biblical mandates. These truths must be embraced if we are to live our lives in right relationship to God.

We are saved *"by grace . . . through faith . . . it is the gift of God: not of works, lest any man should boast"* (Ephesians 2:8-9). We come to Christ strictly on the merits of His shed blood and faith in His redemptive work. Salvation through the blood of Jesus Christ and faith alone is a biblical mandate.

Sometimes people add to salvation and say, "It is faith in Christ plus certain works." Good works emanate from a born again Christian. We cannot earn salvation with good works. We are saved by grace through faith alone and not by any of our additions. That is the clear teaching of the Word of God and it is not up for debate.

The Bible clearly teaches the preexistence of Christ with God in the beginning. It testifies to Christ's death, burial and resurrection. It prophecies His return. These are biblical mandates not up for debate.

THE DANGER

Most troublesome for Christians are the personal convictions and opinions masquerading as biblical mandates. We run into trouble when we attempt to make biblical mandates out of things which do not qualify as mandates. We can elevate our own ideas and try to force them into areas where they do not belong and impose them on other people. By exalting our opinions to a place of high value, we devalue true biblical mandates, as Mark 7:9-13 states:

> "And he said unto them, 'Full well ye reject the commandment of God, that ye may keep your own tradition. For Moses said, "Honour thy father and thy mother; and, Whoso curseth father or mother, let him die the death:" But ye say, "If a man shall say to his father or mother, It is Corban, that is to say, a gift, by whatsoever thou mightest be profited by me; he shall be free." And ye suffer him no more to do ought for his father or his mother; making the word of God of none effect through your tradition, which ye have delivered: and many such like things do ye.'"

Confusion permeates churches that do not understand these distinctions. It is important to draw lines, but we should make sure the things we call biblical mandates really are absolute, clear commands from Scripture.

Here is a good example of a personal conviction or a community standard being "shoehorned" into a wrong category. Some teachers read Deuteronomy 22:5 and decide women cannot wear slacks. It is absolute sin, they say. Deuteronomy 22:5 does say women shall not wear men's clothing and men shall not wear women's clothing, but does the Scripture forbid women wearing slacks?

The unisex trend in the world today blurs the lines between the sexes, especially in fashion. The church even feels pressure to accommodate the trend. Most of us agree the sexes should be identifiable from each other. Scriptures such as 1 Corinthians 11:14-15 and 1 Peter 3:7 maintain a distinction between the sexes, and Romans 1:26-27 and other New Testament verses oppose effeminate behavior in men and masculine behavior in women. However, if we take the Deuteronomy passage as a biblical mandate which bans women in slacks, then to follow proper hermeneutical principles, we have to give equal importance to the rest of the chapter. The same chapter bans clothing made from mixed fiber, such as wool and linen woven together. Have some clothes that might need to be thrown away, then? When establishing standards in the church we cannot pick and choose among the Scriptures to find a few we accept. We must be very careful in this area. A wise person will consider other biblical principles that apply to the areas of dress that focus on maintaining a woman's dignity and beauty.

DRINKING WINE

Is drinking wine forbidden by an absolute biblical mandate? If we go to Italy, we will find genuine believers drinking wine with their meals. It is very customary. In Germany we would find genuine believers with a glass of beer. They do not see a thing wrong with it.

In the southern United States several years ago, most conservative

Christians would never smoke a cigarette, but they had no qualms about chewing tobacco. At tent meetings in the south, I personally cleaned many sawdust floors with tobacco spit all over them.

Allowing differences and variety does not mean we live without limits or lines. We need the help of the Holy Spirit to determine where the lines should be drawn, how they should be drawn, and who they will affect.

DEALING WITH DIFFERENCES

Where God allows variety and liberty, general biblical principles guide Christian behavior. A believer draws godly attitudes and character from these principles. These attitudes equip the believer to respond with Christlike actions when personal opinions, preferences, and convictions clash. Where mandates are not available, principles help Christians walk in line with the truth of the Gospel, deal with differences, and maintain unity.

Without lines or principles to follow, chaos and anarchy rule and people get hurt. Believers who enjoy variety sooner or later collide with each other. The liberty of one man offends another.

Romans 14 shows believers with different personal convictions how to relate to each other to avoid conflicts. That same chapter shows us how to fulfill the Golden Rule, *"Therefore all things whatsoever ye would that men should do to you, do ye even so to them"* (Matthew 7:12). Romans 14 shows us how to fulfill the second greatest commandment, *"Thou shalt love thy neighbour as thyself"* (Matthew 22:39).

Here are nine principles from Romans 14 that provide guidelines for us to follow as we deal with differences between believers:

1. Receive the Weak Brother.

At the church at Rome, some believers did not eat meat. Some chose to eat only vegetables. According to the original Greek text, a quarrel

(Greek: *dialogismos*) erupted over thoughts and opinions. The apostle Paul found no fault with the personal convictions of either party and allowed them the liberty to eat whatever they chose. However, he warned them not to confuse a personal conviction with a biblical mandate.

Paul drew a line separating the two issues and warned them not to think their personal convictions about diet had any impact on their salvation, which clear biblical teaching describes as a gift. Abstaining from meat does not earn anyone's salvation. Paul restrained both sides from substituting their personal opinions for faith in Christ as a means of receiving salvation.

Rigid restrictions against eating meat marked the man weak in faith. Where faith is weak, saints take a legalistic approach to life. Under a legalistic system, people learn to earn acceptance and approval by their works, but it is always wrong to make rules and regulations as a means of salvation. In fact, it is heresy. At the church in Rome, believers who had been raised under Judaism had a tendency toward legalism. Their value system had been built on hundreds of restrictions placed on their lives under the Old Testament economy.

Romans 14:1 charges us to receive one who is weak in the faith. We are to welcome him and accept him just as God welcomes and accepts us. God receives us graciously. When a brother makes personal choices in life different from the choices you have made but not in violation of biblical mandates, receive him without criticism, argument, or judgment. Paul told both these men, "Do not judge one another. Allow God to judge because He is the judge of all" (paraphrased).

2. Do Not Despise and Judge Others.

Paul told the weaker saint and the stronger one not to view each other with contempt (see Romans 14:3-4). God Himself has received both of them. Both are the Lord's servants. Both are accepted in the beloved. God is at work in both of their lives. The Bible says, *"he which hath begun a good work in you will perform it"* (Philippians 1:6), and *"[I] am persuaded that he is able to keep that which I have committed unto him against that day"* (2 Timothy 1:12).

God keeps both strong and weak saints and makes both complete. Both have a secure position in the Lord. Their works do not keep them or make them complete. They are complete in the Lord and should not look down on each other.

3. Be Fully Persuaded of Right and Wrong Behavior.

If a believer holds a personal conviction, he must have inner peace and confidence that his conviction is pure. Others will not necessarily hold the same conviction, so he must be *"fully persuaded in his own mind"* (Romans 14:5).

In Rome, believers in the church differed over how to observe the Sabbath. Hot debate centered on whether one day had special significance or whether every day was the same. Paul did not condemn the celebration of a certain day. He cautioned against worship of the day itself and emphasized worship of the Lord regardless of the preferred day.

I think the strong position sees every day as the Lord's day. To a Christian, every day is the same. Every day is the day the Lord has made. Every day is special.

4. Watch What We Do.

We are to exercise care in our conduct toward others. The saint with whom we have differences also belongs to the Lord. Christ died for both weak and strong saints. Both are accepted by God (see Romans 14:8).

5. Leave the Judgment to God.

Everyone will stand before God's judgment seat and will give an account of himself to the Lord (see Romans 14:10-12). God will judge all by His standards so we are not to look down on another person who does not measure up to our standards. We must allow the Lord to judge. We must be willing to receive those with other views in the Lord.

The person who has Christian liberty has no problem leaving the judgment to God. He allows God, in His infinite wisdom, to settle the problem.

6. Lay No Stumbling Blocks in the Paths of Others.

We need to judge our own conduct. We should ask ourselves, "Am I a stumbling block, a trap, a snare, or an obstacle that causes someone else to sin?" Our job is not to justify our conduct by comparing it to others' conduct. Our job is to ask ourselves, "Am I hurting my brother?"

Romans 14:13-15 gives three guidelines to help us judge ourselves and our conduct. First, respect other Christians' convictions. They love God as much as we do, so we cannot question their convictions.

Second, do not destroy your brother with your liberty. The Bible says we must walk in love toward our brother (Romans 14:15). We are not to distress or grieve him. It is frightening to think our liberty actually could destroy a brother, a sister, a child, a young person, or a teenager.

Third, handle your liberty in a faithful, responsible way. All things are pure in themselves (Romans 14:14), but man perverts pure things. He makes them impure, evil and destructive by irresponsible handling.

7. Give No Occasion for Criticism.

Liberty can be abused. Christian brothers and sisters can be tripped up by our liberty when we seek our own pleasures and desires more than we seek the kingdom of God. If other believers do not share our liberty, they will not view our conduct as balanced and acceptable before God (see Romans 14:16). The kingdom of God is our first concern, and we are to put the spiritual welfare of others before our own pleasures.

Strong believers should be willing to sacrifice a degree of their liberty to help weak believers. Strong believers may enjoy their liberty with a clear conscience, but if their liberty causes their brother to fall, they are to avoid the liberty that brought the weaker brother down.

8. Pursue Things That Bring Peace and Edification.

If our first priority is the kingdom of God and His righteousness, we will seek to edify a weak brother. We will not do anything to bring confusion to his spirit or mind. We will say, "I am going to help him stand. I will not tear him down by taking liberties in things to which he objects."

The Bible says we are to *"live peaceably with all men"* (Romans 12:18), and that we are to edify or build up one another (see Romans 14:19). This will not put us in bondage if our priorities are right.

Because Paul loved his brethren, he surrendered his liberty and made a concession. In a sense, he said, "If eating meat will hurt my brother, I am not going to eat any more hamburgers or pork burgers until the world ends. Take it off my menu" (see 1 Corinthians 8:13). Paul realized weak saints could not handle his liberty.

9. Do Not Condemn Yourself.

"Happy is he that condemneth not himself in that thing which he alloweth." (Romans 14:22)

Do you feel liberty allows you to do a particular thing you know offends another segment of God's people? Here are three ways to keep yourself from being self-condemned:

1. Keep Your Faith.

Your activity must be acceptable to God and you must be able to do it in faith. *"Whatsoever is not of faith is sin"* (Romans 14:23). If you can offer this activity to God with thanksgiving then you can do it. That is where you start, and that eliminates a lot of the questionable areas.

If God does not mind you doing it, but it offends others, then Romans 14:22 directs you to do it privately before God. In other words, you cannot publicly parade it. Such behavior is not hypocritical. It is loving your brother and protecting his weakness. It is protecting his conscience and preventing him from stumbling over your liberty.

2. Do Not Go Against Your Own Conscience.

If your conscience says an activity is wrong, you cannot do it in faith. Do not condemn yourself by violating your conscience. Can you give thanks for the activity? Can you pray before you read it, put it on, watch it, or do it? If so, your conscience is clear before God. Remember, your children and your spouse will be influenced by what you do and by what you allow in your home.

3. Act on Faith from a Conviction that God Approves of the Activity.

Make your behavior consistent with your confession. Some would like to let their liberty rip through the church. They would like to say, "Let the weak fall if they cannot stand. I am not going to be legalistic like they are. I believe that Jesus saves and it does not really matter about my activities. All that matters is just Jesus and me. Church, get out of my way."

The Lord is positioning you to reach the harvest. You have to be very careful that your personal lives do not block the harvest. You cannot cause a brother or sister to stumble. You cannot cause the unbeliever to stumble. You are your brother's keeper.

PERSONAL CONVICTIONS

God gives personal disciplines to His followers. He does not lead all Christians in identical paths. He gives a word of direction to some that is different from the word He gives to others. Biblical mandates apply to everyone equally, yet God creates differing but compatible "paths of righteousness," on which we walk through life (see Proverbs 2:20; 3:6). It is a strictly personal arrangement. Our walk with God is determined by whether we will accept personal disciplines and personal convictions that are just between us and God. Here are some examples of personal convictions from the Bible and modern society.

SAMSON

God asked Samson to do something no one else was asked to do. *"Now therefore beware, I pray thee, and drink not wine nor strong drink, and eat not any unclean thing . . . and no razor shall come on [your] head"* (Judges 13:4-5). This discipline was not given to everyone in Samson's day. It was a personal discipline given to Samson and he accepted it.

DANIEL

God gave Daniel personal convictions. Daniel was a Jew of the tribe of Judah captured by King Nebuchadnezzar's army and taken to Babylon. When he and other young Hebrew leaders were selected for training in Nebuchadnezzar's palace, Daniel faced a challenge to one of his personal convictions. He was given food and wine from the king's table and told to eat. At the time, Daniel did not eat meat. He ate only vegetables and drank water.

Daniel purposed in his heart that he would not defile himself with the portion of the king's delicacies, nor with the wine which he drank; therefore he requested of the chief of the eunuchs that he might not defile himself (see Daniel 1:8).

Daniel was not attempting to press his convictions on anyone else. He did not claim a biblical mandate for his position. God had not taken all meats or wine out of the Hebrew diet. Meat from certain unclean animals was off limits, but we do not know what was on the royal menu offered to Daniel. This was Daniel's own personal conviction. When he went into captivity, Daniel agreed before God to keep certain standards. He simply said, "I have purposed in my heart not to eat from the king's table. I do not want his wine. I do not want his meat. Just let me have some vegetables."

TELEVISION

Some Christians believe television is so corrupt it should not be in a believer's home. That is their personal conviction, but they should not condemn the saint who has a television. Likewise, the saint with a television set should not condemn Christians who abstain from watching one. The television watcher should not accuse others of weak faith, implying, "They just cannot handle it and I can."

EDUCATION

Some parents put their children in public school and believe their children should be "salt" and "light" in the public system. Some parents believe in Christian schools and some in home school. We cannot condemn families who school their children differently than we do. We should allow our convictions to rule our decisions.

DRAW LINES EARLY

Lines should be drawn well in advance of the time of testing. Worldly pressure and temptation come and catch believers off guard. Personal convictions are a well-prepared line of defense for the believer against the influence and temptations of this present age.

We must set our limits before we get in the heat of battle. Do not postpone action thinking, "When I am faced with pressure or temptation, then I'll draw the line." At that point, it is too late. We are not prepared to resist the pressure and fight the tempter.

FAMILY COMMUNITY STANDARDS

Convictions, opinions and preferences vary from person to person and from family to family. They also vary from generation to generation, and where God allows for liberty and variety, we must also.

In my own home, I did not want my four daughters to wear earrings. It was my personal conviction. I would have a hard time finding a biblical mandate saying women should not wear earrings. I drew that line and set the standard in my own home based on my personal convictions. It was never a community standard in the church. In thirty years of pastoring, I have never asked women in the church not to wear earrings. But my daughters were subject to my family community standard and were required to follow that.

Parents, you have a biblical mandate to set community standards in your own homes based on your personal convictions. It is your privilege, but do not judge other families if they do not have the same personal convictions or standards.

COMMUNITY STANDARDS

"No Shoes, No Shirt, No Service." We see the signs in restaurant windows. When we walk into a restaurant, we are submitting to a community standard. The restaurant owner has defined acceptable behavior in his "community" and has set the standards by placing a sign in the window.

If we take a job in the bank, our boss will tell us to dress nicely. If we refuse, we violate a community standard and our employment there may come to an abrupt halt.

If we join the police force, the chief will expect us to wear a uniform and behave in a certain way because those are community standards.

Normal living requires community standards to bring order. A home, church, business, or group of any kind that does not have community standards will not last long. It will not survive. Chaos and anarchy will spell the end of the group.

LEADERS SET STANDARDS

God puts leaders in every community to guide and give directions to the people in it. God gives leaders the authority to take care of the community and to set standards. God supports and respects that leadership.

In the home, dad and mom have the right to prayerfully set community standards. That is their job. A home is a community and parental authority is confirmed by biblical mandate. *"Honour thy father and thy mother . . ."* (Exodus 20:12). *"Children, obey your parents in the Lord: for this is right"* (Ephesians 6:1).

Parents do not need a scripture to say, "When you go out tonight, I want to know where you are, who you are seeing and when you will be back." Parents do not need to defend their standards for bedtime, curfew, table manners, or dish washing with specific Scriptures. Instead, parents' judgements are backed by their biblically-mandated general authority to care for their families.

Without standards, family members do what they want when they want, wear what they want, eat, sleep, come, and go when they want. Homes without standards are in chaos. Family members guard only their own interests and bite at one another. God does not want that for our homes.

CHURCH LEADERS

To Jesus the most important thing on the face of the earth is the church. The church is a community, a family, the body of Christ set together by the Holy Spirit. It is not just a crowd coming together to watch a performance. The church is a society.

In the church, elders prayerfully set community standards under the authority of Scripture set forth by New Testament government principles.

"Obey them that have the rule over you, and submit yourselves: for they watch for your souls, as they that must give account, that they may do it with joy, and not with grief: for that is unprofitable for you." (Hebrews 13:17)

These verses do not refer to obeying the Bible. They refer to obeying and esteeming church leaders. For church life to flow smoothly, spiritual leaders should set standards and the fellowship of believers should respect those standards and respond to them. Community standards bring order, and order gives people security. As in the family, standards set by church leaders cannot always be supported by specific Scriptures.

I responded to the elders in my first illustration who wanted me to take off my ring. Their community standard opposed jewelry. They did not have a biblical mandate banning jewelry, but they had a biblical mandate to set standards of behavior in their local church, and I respected their judgment.

If the church did not have community standards, it would not have order. No one would know when to meet, when not to meet, who to see, where to call, and how to get involved. It would be total anarchy. Living without a set of standards places the church in danger. Any church that does not set community standards will not last long. It will not survive when believers with differences begin biting and devouring one another.

STANDARDS CHANGE

God's laws do not change, but where God allows variety, men draw lines that require change from time to time. Personal convictions and community standards do not have the same permanence as biblical standards. As time passes, lines drawn by men must gradually be readjusted.

We have watched beards and mustaches become accepted and worn by well-groomed men. In 1969 when the hippie revolt took place, kids broke out of the Judeo-Christian ethic and hit the streets. Young people wore beads, long hair, and every weird thing that would bring a reaction from their parents or peers.

At that time, our church had a community standard discouraging beards. We were training young people at the bible college and did not allow young men to wear beards or long hair. We told them to submit to the community standard if they planned on being a leader in the house of God. We got a lot of reaction, but in that day a beard was considered by many to be a mark of open rebellion. Christians are not to identify with rebellion. Rebellion put Christ on the cross.

As time went on, these lines changed. Now beards no longer symbolize rebellion. They are a normal part of society. Many men in our church wear beards. Now we simply encourage those who desire leadership to keep their beards well groomed.

TIMOTHY AND TITUS

We see the apostle Paul bend to accommodate a community standard in the book of Acts when he instructs Timothy to be circumcised. Paul had just argued against requiring circumcision for Gentile believers (see Acts 15:5,12), yet he had Timothy circumcised before they embarked on a missionary journey (see Acts 16:3). Paul's personal conviction was that *"in Christ Jesus neither circumcision availeth any thing, nor uncircumcision"* (Galatians 6:15), but he and Timothy were going to work among non-Christian Jews. Paul knew if Timothy was not circumcised, it would cause an unnecessary controversy and hinder the evangelistic work. The unsaved Jewish audience would not listen to the Gospel message from an uncircumcised man. Timothy had Jewish blood through his mother and the Jews would question his loyalty to Israel if he was not circumcised. Having Timothy circumcised was a recognition of the Jews' community standard and Paul's willingness to be *"all things to all men"* (1 Corinthians 9:22).

Timothy knew he was not being circumcised to be saved. This was not a religious work to win acceptance from God. It was not done to honor the rite of circumcision. It was done to eliminate the potential controversy over a community standard so the Jews would hear the Gospel.

Titus, on the other hand, was not compelled to be circumcised by Paul or by pressure from other apostles (see Galatians 2:1-3). Titus was a Greek. He was sent to build a church in Crete, which is not a Jewish area. He preached to a Gentile culture which exerted no pressure on him to adopt a Jewish custom.

SETTLING DIFFERENCES

In our church we have tried to keep nonessentials and misunderstandings from causing division between Christian brothers and sisters. Misunderstanding often lies at the heart of differences and disagreements. A few minutes or, in some cases, a few hours of conversation usually put most of these differences to rest. How can two walk together unless they agree (see Amos 3:3)? And how can they agree if they do not take the time to try to understand each other?

When someone does not understand or agree with a community standard or anything taught in their church, they should not just separate from the church.

The best way to resolve the difference is to begin by talking to the local church leadership. Discuss the difference. Seriously pray. Ask God to reveal truth to the leadership, then leave it alone. If the leaders do not adopt your particular viewpoint, you still do not need to leave the church, but be quiet about the difference. Do not go around the church spreading your view. The unity of the Body of Christ is critical in God's mind.

Respect and respond to those in authority and do not spread division. It is not proper to go to a church and tell everyone, "I go to church here, but I do not believe what they teach." That behavior contradicts the Word of God. Personal liberty is not more important than the unity of the Body of Christ. If the difference is not resolved, the dissatisfied believer should quietly leave and find a church where the leadership expounds the view he can support.

There are three classes to consider when drawing lines. There are biblical mandates, personal convictions and community standards. Biblical mandates are clear Scriptural principles. Personal convictions are based on our personal response to biblical principles. In determining what the community standards should be, each church will face many differing opinions and will have to make a decision based on how the leadership as a whole views the biblical principles. May God grant us much wisdom as we continue to build the church.

CHAPTER FOUR

Persevering Truth:
Keeping Our Focus

WHAT IS BURNOUT?

While on a summer holiday, I was "burning out" under the sun getting a suntan when the Lord dropped a thought into my mind. He said, "My people should never burn out."

Burnout is the number one reason people leave their careers or change vocations. Pastors vacate their pulpits and missionaries abandon their fields, not because of immorality or any other problem, but because of burnout. People everywhere are becoming so exhausted they simply cannot go on. Needless to say, I was very intrigued when the Lord said, "My people should never suffer from burnout."

All of us want to discover what the remedy for burnout is. But first we must clearly understand the cause. Because we are living in a society filled with stress, the bookstores abound with material on burnout. Often we are told that if we change our lifestyle, quit our jobs, move to another location, or make some other external adjustment, we will be cured from burnout. But is that really the answer?

The problem of burnout is also affecting the church. Yet it seems to me that if everything else is in order, believers need not collapse under the pressures of life as others do. In fact, serving the Lord should be a great source of fulfillment. We all need times of rest and relaxation, but it should not be necessary to become so drained we are forced to quit. Rather God wants us to stay in the fight and continue to bear fruit in the assignment He is given us.

What causes burnout, then? Following are five factors that can cause burnout for us as we serve God:

1. When We Lose God's Perspective for Our Lives

In the midst of our life work we may begin to lose sight of who we are and why we are doing what we are doing. At that point we are no longer seeing life from God's perspective. The normal pressures of life will then begin to drain us with no way of renewing our strength.

All true Christians are followers of Christ. That means they are Christ-centered, not self-centered. The focus of their lives is the kingdom of God and its advancement, not their kingdom and their advancement. But if they are not careful, they could easily become distracted from that focus. At that point it becomes increasingly difficult to see all the various aspects of life from God's perspective, and burnout becomes a possibility for the believer.

Such a person has lost his sense of meaning in life. He has lost track of why he does what he does. Life becomes a matter of grinding it out day after day, and each day has a little less meaning than the day before. That is when burnout begins to happen.

2. When We Lose Our Vision for the Future

When we stop seeing life from God's perspective, we also stop seeing life in the context of the eternal purposes of God. When we look down the road of our lives and see no goals, we will have no clear sense of direction or fulfillment. This makes us even more vulnerable to weakness in the face of pressure.

If we do not sense that the Lord's goals for our life are being fulfilled, we might become frustrated with unfulfilled expectations and create our own goals. It is possible to have personal goals and expectations that have not been given to us by the Lord. Some of our goals may be unattainable because they are our own and not the Lord's. Such goals lead to anxiety, frustration, unfulfillment, and eventually, exhaustion.

As we follow the Lord, He may change our assignment. That means we have to be flexible. But when we are following our own goals and expectations and the Lord tries to change them, we are tempted to become even more frustrated, if not bitter and cynical. That is why the Lord tells us, *"For my thoughts are not your thoughts, neither are your ways my ways, saith the Lord. For as the heavens are higher than the earth, so are my ways higher than your ways, and my thoughts than your thoughts."* (Isaiah 55:8-9).

If we try to live our lives aiming at goals that are not of God, we will not have His grace in meeting them. The only way we can succeed is to conform our ways to God's ways.

3. When We Live Under Stress for Too Long, We Finally Give Up.

If we continue to live long enough under life's pressure without God's perspective and vision for our lives, we will end up physically, emotionally, and spiritually exhausted. God never intended for us to live in a continual state of war. We will always have periodic battles in life, but it is not God's desire for us to be at war all of the time. It is not necessary for us to always be anxious and uptight.

If there is never any real peace, something is wrong. When we are doing the will of God, we seek His kingdom first, we will see the evidence of the kingdom in our lives. *"For the kingdom of God is not meat and drink; but righteousness, and peace, and joy in the Holy Ghost"* (Romans 14:17). Jesus said, *"These things I have spoken unto you, that in me ye might have peace. In the world ye shall have tribulation; but be of good cheer; I have overcome the world,"* (John 16:33). The marks of God's rule in our lives are righteousness, peace, and joy. If we are seeking His kingdom, we will know peace.

As we reach a state of exhaustion, we will be tempted to quit, thinking that quitting will renew our energy. But that is not the answer. If we quit, we will be even further out of God's will and that will lead to another cycle of frustration, anxiety, and exhaustion. When drained and exhausted, we cannot quit. Instead, we must take another look at our lives in the light of God's will and make adjustments to conform more fully with it. When we make those adjustments, our tiredness will be replaced with a godly energy. That energy will help us maintain our work for the kingdom and experience the righteousness, peace, and joy that results from it.

4. When You Serve for the Wrong Reasons

Years ago, one of the faithful members of our congregation began to put me up on a pedestal. He even tried to imitate me in a variety of ways. I did not know what to do about it. Then one day the Lord allowed me to make a bad judgment concerning him. I was unfair to him and he knew it. That pulled the rug out from under him and he nearly collapsed spiritually. He became bitter and disillusioned.

As I prayed about the matter, it seemed as though the Lord showed me what had happened and why. Because the young man was serving the Lord for my approval and not God's, the Lord had to remove me from the pedestal the young man had put me on in order to adjust his motives. The brother would then be free to refocus his attention and his service on the Lord.

Others may serve the Lord to establish their own self-worth. They want to feel important and that is what moves them to serve. This was Martha's dilemma:

"Now it came to pass, as they went, that He entered into a certain village: and a certain woman named Martha received Him into her house. And she had a sister called Mary, which also sat at Jesus' feet, and heard his word. But Martha was cumbered about much serving, and came to Him, and said, 'Lord, dost thou not care that my sister hath left me to serve alone? bid her therefore that she help me.' And Jesus answered and said unto her, 'Martha, Martha, thou are careful and troubled about many things: but one thing is needful; and Mary hath chosen that good part, which shall not be taken away from her.'" (Luke 10:38-42)

Martha's priorities were wrong. She wanted to please the Lord, but pleasing Him involved more than serving Him. It also involved communing with Him.

The phrase "cumbered about" means to be anxious, worried, tied up, and bothered. Martha was serving but she was in bondage to her service. She was hoping to gain the approval of Jesus by serving Him. Instead, He was ignoring her. His response was, "Mary had chosen the good part." He was not implying that Mary should not serve, but rather that Martha's motive for serving should be to please the Lord and not to establish her own self-worth.

Some of us will serve the Lord based upon the needs we see around us. As we do, the burdens we place on our own shoulders can become very heavy and lead us to a place of exhaustion. Just because the need is there does not necessarily mean that God will use us to address that need. Our service should be a result of God's leading to address the needs around us.

Followers of Jesus Christ should focus every aspect of their lives on advancing His kingdom. At work, at school, and at play, everything should be done with God's kingdom in mind. When we lose our focus on God and instead work to win the approval of others or increase self-esteem, then fear, anxiety, and unbelief enters will come to us and lead to the possibility of burnout.

God does not want His church to burn out. He wants us to understand that *"whatsoever you do in word and deed, do it all in the name of the Lord Jesus"* (Colossians 3:17). We must not serve for man's approval, to prove our self-worth, or just because we see a need. We must do it to please God.

5. When We Cannot Handle Failure

If we are self-focused rather than God-focused and things go wrong in our lives, we will not have the grace to overcome those failures. If our lives are centered around comfort or things, when those things are suddenly lost due to some failure, we will be tempted to say, "I am through! I have been serving God and now look what's happened. I quit!"

If we never experienced anything but success, if everything always went our way, what kind of people would we be? How much strength would we really have? I remember attending a pastors' gathering where they were all telling how great their churches were doing. But one pastor was having some serious problems and in his pain said, "Please, give me room to fail!"

We live in a generation where everything is positive. We do not even like to think about failure. But the times when we experience the most growth are times of crisis. When everything was shaken that could be shaken, God was all that remained. If, during times of crisis and failure, we remain confident in the Lord and stand our ground, our roots will go down deeper than ever and we will come out of the night hour with a new level of strength and stability.

HOW TO AVOID BURNOUT

A survey taken among pastors showed that sixty-seven percent of them claimed to be suffering from burnout. In making that claim, they were saying that they had lost their vision, were exhausted, and wanted to get out of the ministry. If the leaders of the church are suffering burnout to this extent, then the members must also be experiencing it.

And yet, it is not necessary for any of God's people to burn out. How can we avoid this currently pervasive problem? Jesus proposed an answer in Matthew:

"Do not gather and heap up and store for yourselves treasures on earth, where moth and rust and worm consume and destroy, and where thieves break through and steal; but gather and heap up and store for yourselves treasures in heaven, where neither moth nor rust nor worm consume and destroy, and where thieves do not break through and steal; for where your treasure is, there will your heart be also. The eye is the lamp of the body. So, if your eye is sound, your entire body will be full of light; but if your eye is unsound, your whole body will be full of darkness. If then the very light in you (your conscience) is darkened, how dense is that darkness! No one can serve two masters; for either he will hate the one and love the other, or he will stand by and be devoted to the one and despise and be against the other. You cannot serve God and mammon (that is, deceitful riches, money, possessions or what is trusted in). Therefore I tell you, stop being perpetually uneasy (anxious and worried) about your life, what you shall eat or what you shall drink, and about your body, what you shall put on. Is not life greater (in quality) than food, and the body (far above and more excellent) than clothing? Look at the birds of the air; they neither sow nor reap nor gather into barns, and yet your

heavenly Father keeps feeding them. Are you not worth more than they? And which of you by worrying and being anxious can add one unit of measure (cubit) to his stature or to the span of his life? And why should you be anxious about clothes? Consider the lilies of the field and learn thoroughly how they grow; they neither toil nor spin; yet I tell you, even Solomon in all his magnificence (excellence, dignity and grace) was not arrayed like one of these. But if God so clothes the grass of the field, which today is alive and green and tomorrow is tossed into the furnace, will He not much more surely clothe you, O you men with little faith? Therefore do not worry and be anxious, saying, What are we going to have to eat? or, What are we goin to have to drink? or, What are we going to have to wear? For the Gentiles (heathen) wish for and crave and diligently seek after all these things; and your heavenly Father well knows that you need them all. But seek for (aim at and strive after) first of all His kingdom, and His righteousness (His way of doing and being right), and then all these things taken together will be given you besides. So do not worry or be anxious about tomorrow, for tomorrow will have worries and anxieties of its own. Sufficient for each day is its own trouble." (Matthew 6:19-34, Amplified Version).

We run the risk of experiencing burnout when we try to face the pressures of life without relying on God's grace and power. All of us face problems in life all of the time. The difference lies in how we respond to those problems. If we respond with a self-centered rather than God-centered attitude, we will end up bearing that pressure alone and may find that we are unable to stand under it. When we focus all of our attention on the unpleasant situations or the seemingly impossible problems we are facing, they will begin to consume our minds, we will lose the eternal perspective, and will eventually crumble under their weight.

Just making changes will not solve the problem. We can change jobs, change the town we are living in, change churches, change anything and everything, but as long as our focus is wrong, we will burn out again, in that new job, new town, or new church.

If anybody had sufficient reason to burn out, it was the apostle Paul. Look at how he handled stress:

"But in all things approving ourselves as the ministers of God, in much patience, in afflictions, in necessities, in distresses, in stripes, in imprisonments, in tumults, in labours, in watchings, in fastings; by pureness, by knowledge, by longsuffering, by kindness, by the Holy Ghost, by love unfeigned, by the word of truth, by the power of God, by the armour of righteousness on the right hand and on the left, by honour and dishonour, by evil report and good report: as deceivers, and yet true; as unknown, and yet well known; as dying, and, behold, we live; as chastened, and not killed; as sorrowful, yet always rejoicing; as poor, yet making many rich; as having nothing, and yet possessing all things." (2 Corinthians 6:4-10)

Due to his great faith, Paul readily admitted that he had problems and even listed them: "I have a lot of distress, I have been beaten and imprisoned, I have experienced conflicts and struggles of all kinds, I have lost sleep and gone without food...." But he seems to forget his list of difficulties as he focuses on other aspects of his life. Indeed, it is Paul's focus on these other things that is Paul's secret—his life was focused on the Holy Spirit, the Word of God, the power of God, the spiritual weapons God had given him, and the love of God. It was these things that kept him on course. If his eyes had just been focused on his many problems he would have collapsed under the weight of them. Paul gives his secret again in 2 Timothy 4:7. *"I have fought a good fight,*

I have finished my course, I have kept the faith." He knew what he was fighting for and where he was going—that is what kept him from burning out.

God wants us to be able to see all of life from His perspective. God has given us an eternal destiny in His kingdom. If we will put His kingdom first, we will be able to stay on course, experience the grace and power of the Lord, be guided by the Word of God, have the joy of the Lord fill and strengthen our souls, and never burn out. Every day will be a fresh opportunity to serve the Lord and make a difference in our generation.

Here are six specific things we can do to avoid burnout:

1. Learn to Serve.

If we live a self-centered, self-serving life, we will run the risk of burning out. The Lord has poured out His love and Spirit upon us, He has given us the presence and gifts of His Holy Spirit for a purpose. He has redeemed us and abundantly blessed us so that we can release those blessings to others. Love is not love until it is given away. In other words, like Jesus Christ, we exist to serve others. If we refuse to serve, we will have no fulfillment in life and will soon begin to weary of it.

The world is full of self-serving people. They push drugs, strive to climb the corporate ladder, pursue free sex and pleasures of all kind—with the entire focus of their lives being to serve themselves. As long as they live only to serve themselves, they will have no happiness, fulfillment, or ability to avoid burnout.

In Mark 10:43, Jesus said that the greatest calling in life is to be a servant. The greatest calling is not that of the apostle, the prophet, the evangelist, pastor or teacher, but the servant. The man or woman who really wants to find greatness and fulfillment in life must be a servant.

2. Learn to Give.

Paul taught that if we are going to avoid burnout and receive the grace and blessings of the Lord, we need to give. Notice 2 Corinthians 9:6-8:

> *"But this I say, He which soweth sparingly shall reap also sparingly; and he which soweth bountifully shall reap also bountifully. Every man according as he purposeth in his heart, so let him give; not grudgingly, or of necessity: for God loveth a cheerful giver. And God is able to make all grace abound toward you; that ye, always having all sufficiency in all things, may abound to every good work."*

If we want to receive God's blessings in our lives, we must become a channel of blessing to others; and as we release those blessings, God will release even more blessings to us. That was the principle by which Jesus lived His life and He was able to bring many sons to glory.

If you are going to avoid burnout, you must learn to give. Give hilariously! Give with joy! Give because the Spirit of Christ and the love of God are in you and flowing out of you to others.

3. Learn to Live One Day at a Time.

If we are living a kingdom life, we will have goals and dreams. But if we are constantly worrying and fretting, "What's going to happen to the economy, what's going to happen in the elections, what about my Social Security," we will be violating the principle of God's Word. From Matthew 6:34, we can hear Jesus saying, "You take care of today; do not worry about tomorrow. When you get to tomorrow, I'll be with you. You do not have to bank your future on the economy of America; you bank your future on Me. I'll be with you."

Every day our confession should be, *"This is the day the Lord hath made"* (Psalm 118:24). Every day is the first day of the rest of our lives. If we stumble today, tomorrow is a brand new day. When we get to tomorrow, we must make that day count. We can make every day an opportunity to serve the Lord and bring Him glory. He will not give us grace for the future, only the present. Today is the day we have to serve and give with the strength God will provide, and if we do, we will not burn out.

4. Never Grow Bitter.

Accumulating offenses from the past will cause us to burn out. When we become bitter by holding onto offenses, we will lose our joy, the sense of the presence of the Lord, and the ability to face the pressures of life.

Bitterness is a greater enemy than the original offense. It is worse than our original response to that offense. It ties up our spirit and keeps us in bondage to the past. It is impossible to overcome in life and be bitter. It is a trap that will destroy us.

As long as we have any contact with people, we are going to be offended. But rather than allowing ourselves to become bitter, we should do as Jesus taught: love our enemies and bless those that persecute us. In this way we will be free in our spirit and free from burnout.

If we allow bitterness to grow within us, we become people who say, "Every time I go to help people, they spit on me and walk all over me, so I am not going to get involved with people any more!" But the mission of the kingdom of God and our purpose in life is to reach out to people with the love of God! Satan would like nothing more than to make us bitter, discouraged, and disillusioned until we refuse to have anything more to do with people (especially certain people). Then we will turn inward and begin to focus on living for ourselves until the light of God's love grows dimmer and dimmer and finally goes out altogether. Burnout is avoided as harboring bitterness is avoided.

5. Stay in the Will of God.

We must keep our eyes on the purpose of God for our lives. There are many people who start to pursue God's will but then suddenly change course. They see the obstacles along the way but do not see God's ability to lift them above those obstacles. The result is that they eventually get off track.

Before we make any course adjustments in our lives we need to ask ourselves this question: "Will this advance the kingdom of God?" If the answer is not a clear "Yes!" then we must not make that change.

James wrote:

"Go to now, ye that say, Today or tomorrow we will go into such a city, and continue there a year, and buy and sell, and get gain: Whereas ye know not what shall be on the morrow . . . For that ye ought to say, If the Lord will, we shall live, and do this, or that." (James 4:13-15)

Every decision, action, and change must be centered in the will of God. If we seek first the kingdom of God and His righteousness, then all these things will be added to us as well (see Matthew 6:33).

6. Spend Quality Time with the Lord.

The life of the church is wonderful. Assembling together for worship, prayer, teaching, and fellowship is essential to our spiritual health. But the most important element in maintaining our spiritual life is our personal relationship with the Lord. The only way we can have such a relationship is to spend quality time with Him in prayer and mediation on His Word.

Paul put it this way:

"Be careful for nothing; but in every thing by prayer and supplication with thanksgiving let your requests be made known unto

God. And the peace of God, which passeth all understanding,
shall keep your hearts and minds through Christ Jesus."
(Philippians 4:6-7)

If we do not have a vital daily spiritual connection with Jesus
Christ, we will not be able to serve consistently, give joyfully, walk by
faith one day at a time, guard our hearts from bitterness, or keep our
eyes focused on the will of God for our lives. Without consistent daily
communion with the Lord we will be unable to avoid burnout.

Jesus is the One who gives us strength, keeps our spirits free, fills
us with joy, gives us His vision for our lives, and gives us daily grace. If
we learn to abide with Jesus, we will never burn out.

The Attitude of Faith

Avoiding burnout is better than curing it. If we are going to successful-
ly avoid burnout, we must learn how to handle stress and pressure
with the weapons of God and by living according to the principles of
God's Word.

Learning how to handle stress depends on our attitude toward it.
Stress is increasing in our day. The Bible speaks about the pressures of
the last days—men running to and fro and their hearts failing them for
fear. Remember that sixty-seven percent of the pastors once polled in a
national survey said they were suffering from burnout. The number
one reason why people leave their jobs, their homes, and even their
families, is burnout and the belief that leaving will cure them. But quitting will only make matters worse.

We have already looked at six ways to avoid burnout. Here is a seventh:

7. Develop a Faith Attitude Toward Life.

Approaching life with the attitude of faith releases the power and provision of God. Without a faith attitude, without a believing heart, burnout becomes a distinct possibility.

The Bible speaks about faith as a gift in 1 Corinthians 12. The Bible speaks of faith as fruit in Galatians 5. A gift is something we have no responsibility for. It is simply given to us by God. The gift of faith is a word of faith that is dropped into our hearts when facing a particular situation. When we are facing a mountain and it seems impossible to deal with, God, in His sovereignty, speaks a word of faith into our hearts that, when believed, gives us the divine ability to move that mountain.

Some people only occasionally experience this kind of faith. They go from mountain to mountain with words of faith from the Holy Spirit, but in the valleys they walk in fear, doubt, and unbelief. They doubt God's Word and God's faithfulness. They worry and complain. And still, when they are backed into a corner, God puts a word in their heart and in their mouth and they are able to overcome.

Faith as a fruit is not just something that happens to us. The fruit of faith is something that grows, something that develops over a lifetime, something we base our lives on.

The Bible says that the just, the justified ones, live by faith. This involves a continuous lifestyle of faith. The gift of faith is wonderful, but we cannot live a consistently overcoming life unless we have the fruit of faith (the attitude of faith) in our hearts. We need to walk by faith.

To develop an attitude of faith we must understand:

1. The Power of a Believing Heart.

The more we believe God, the stronger our faith becomes. Faith is like a muscle. If we use it on an ongoing basis, it gets stronger. If we exercise faith only occasionally and try to move too large a mountain, we will not succeed and probably strain the muscle of our faith in the process. But if we are walking by faith all of the time, when a trial does come our way, we will be able to face it and overcome it.

Romans 12:2 says, *"And be not conformed to this world: but be ye transformed by the renewing of your mind, that ye may prove what is that good, and acceptable, and perfect, will of God."* Paul is telling us that if there is any area of our lives that is not completely submitted to the lordship of Christ, if doing God's will is not the center of our lives, we need to have our minds renewed so they will conform to the mind of Christ.

He then goes on to say, *"For I say, through the grace given unto me, to every man that is among you, not to think of himself more highly than he ought to think; but to think soberly, according as God hath dealt to every man the measure of faith"* (Romans 12:3). Everyone has been given a measure of faith. Everyone has within him the ability to believe and trust the Lord in every situation. If our minds are renewed according to the knowledge of God, we will know we have true faith within and will be ready to begin to walk by faith, develop our faith, and see it grow strong.

Jesus certainly recognized that some had weak or little faith while others had strong faith. He often asked, "Where is your faith?" or said, "Your faith has healed you." There are stages and levels of faith and there is no question the Lord wants each of us to reach a level of great faith. We can have great faith if we consistently walk by faith and commit ourselves to developing strong faith.

Hebrews 11:6 says, *"But without faith it is impossible to please him."* Faith is not just a nice luxury that the deeply spiritual people develop. Faith is the foundation and center of our walk with the Lord. Everything happens in the kingdom of God according to our faith. Faith is the thing that propels us through life. It is faith that enables us to rise above mountains and pass through valleys. Faith keeps us on the course the Lord has set for us. The life and walk of faith will keep us from ever burning out. It is no wonder that our enemy attacks us at the point of our faith.

2. The Loss of an Unbelieving Heart.

Moses recorded ten different occasions when Israel murmured against God in the wilderness. Their murmuring, complaining, and negative attitude was simply an evidence of unbelief in their hearts. The writer to the Hebrews remarked:

> *"Wherefore I was grieved with that generation, and said, 'They do always err in their heart; and they have not known my ways.' So I sware in my wrath, 'They shall not enter into my rest. Take heed, brethren, lest there be in any of you an evil heart of unbelief."'* (Numbers 3:10-12)

The attitude of murmuring is a sign of an evil heart. When we begin to murmur, it shows that we have turned our focus away from the Lord and become convinced that God has forsaken us—that our situation is hopeless. It is then that our souls become unstable and our lives begin to wander away from God's will. No wonder unbelief is said to come from an evil heart.

A person with an attitude of faith is still a realist. However, he clearly understands that if he is going to be able to rise above his trying circumstances, he must keep his mind and his faith centered on Christ and expect that the Lord will strengthen him and enable him to overcome. But if he allows himself to focus on the negative circumstances and begin to murmur and complain, his heart will fill with fear and unbelief and he will receive no strength or overcoming power from the Lord.

3. The Results of a Believing Heart.

"He that believeth on Him is not condemned" (John 3:18). The believer is no longer subject to the judgment of God. He has been forgiven, cleansed, and is a child of God. But if someone persists in his unbelief, there is no forgiveness for him. An unbeliever is living in his sins. All he will ever know is unrighteousness and death. Righteousness and life is the portion of the believer.

"He that believeth on the Son of God hath the witness in himself" (1 John 5:10). The one who really has faith in God has within himself the witness of the Holy Spirit. His heart and mind are filled with assurance and confidence in the Lord. He knows that the righteousness of Christ belongs to him. Believers are to be the most confident people in the world because of their faith in God. An attitude of unbelief only results in fear, uncertainty, and instability in every area of life.

"These things have I written unto you that believe on the name of the Son of God; that ye may know that ye have eternal life" (1 John 5:13). The believer not only has eternal life, he knows he has eternal life. He is able to truly enjoy this life as well as look forward to never ending life to come in the presence of the Lord. He is able to experience a little bit of heaven on the way to heaven. The one with a heart of unbelief knows only doubt, anxiety, and struggle in his attempt to make sense out of his life. True abundant life belongs only to the believer.

"This is the victory that overcometh the world, even our faith" (1 John 5:4). If we have an attitude of faith, we will receive the grace and strength to overcome anything the world throws at us. A daily lifestyle of faith enables us to rise above the pressures of life and therefore keeps us from burning out. The one with unbelief has no strength but his own to turn to and may soon collapse under the weight of the world.

"Whatsoever is not of faith is sin" (Romans 14:23). Everyone knows that lying and stealing are sins. But the essence of sin is unbelief. Sin is a refusal to accept God's Word as our standard in life and a commitment to live according to our own standards. And the wages of sin is death.

The men and women of God that reach God's goals for their lives are those who have a faith attitude. They put all their confidence in God and His Word, they are able to see the hand of the Lord in every situation, and as a result, when the pressures of life press in upon them, they are able to believe God, pass through the wilderness, and enter into the land the Lord has promised them.

4. The Perseverance of a Believing Heart.

What would happen if, in the midst of a real crisis, we prayed, sought the Lord continually, and then nothing happened? What if we then went to our elders to find help for the crisis and they only rebuked us and told us to go home and forget it? What if we sought out the counsel of a godly leader and he said, "Look, you aren't even in the right church—you aren't a part of God's house at all." What would we do? Would we eventually give up and sink down in unbelief?

In Matthew, a woman's faith was challenged in just that way:

"And, behold a woman of Canaan came out of the same coasts, and cried unto him, saying, 'Have mercy on me, O Lord, thou Son of David; my daughter is grievously vexed with a devil.' But he answered her not a word. And his disciples came and besought him, saying, 'Send her away; for she crieth after us.' But he answered and said, 'I am not sent but unto the lost sheep of the house of Israel.' Then came she and worshipped him, saying, 'Lord, help me.' But he answered and said, 'It is not meet to take the children's bread, and to cast it to dogs.' And she said, 'Truth, Lord: yet the dogs eat of the crumbs which fall from their masters'

table.' Then Jesus answered and said unto her, 'O woman, great is thy faith: be it unto thee even as thou wilt.' And her daughter was made whole from that very hour." (Matthew 15:22-28)

This Gentile woman was a powerful example of genuine faith–faith that overcame all obstacles and pressed on to obtain the will and provision of God.

God has designed all men to have such faith. God never created man to be an unbeliever. He intended us to live life with an attitude of faith, not one of unbelief and murmuring. Unbelief is unnatural, it is unhealthy; it will pull us down and eventually destroy us. God designed our souls to be full of faith, and it is an attitude of faith that will lead us on into the fulfillment of His purpose for our lives.

Please understand that this faith I am referring to is not just a mental attitude. True faith is a result of our relationship with God. Faith is a life of dependence on God and it keeps us from ever being separated from Him–not even by tribulations, trials, pressures, or stress.

I bank my eternal life on this one factor–I am a believer. When I come to the moment of death, it does not move me. Even though I die, I am still going to trust Him. That is the attitude of the believer, the attitude that overcomes and enables us to avoid burnout.

If we are going to live a godly life in Jesus Christ, we will never be free from the pressures and stresses of life. In fact, the Scriptures declare that they are going to increase in the last days. But more than that, God wants our faith to increase in the last days. Are we going to accept the challenge of developing a strong attitude of faith? Is the Lord going to say of us, "There is a man or woman of great faith–a person who pleases me?" Without faith it is impossible to please God. Let's determine to accept the challenge and be the generation of believers that will overcome and never burn out! Great churches are known for such stamina.

CHAPTER FIVE

Fundamental Truth:
Repentance

THE MEANING OF REPENTANCE

Today more than ever, I am convinced that we build our lives carefully according to the pattern of God's Word. To build according to the pattern, we must build on God's foundation. Without a strong foundation in our lives, we will either be limited in how largely we can build or our building will end up having cracks in it and may eventually crumble and fall.

Chapter two in Acts gives us a very detailed plan and design for our foundation. It gives us a clear pattern for coming to the Lord, making Him our Lord and Savior, knowing His ways, and walking in victory. After Peter preached on the Day of Pentecost, those who listened realized they had not accepted Jesus as the promised Messiah. They rejected the prophetic word that had come to them from the Old Testament. That word had been fulfilled in Jesus, the Messiah, whom they had crucified, and now they were mightily convicted in their hearts. Their response became the first step in the pattern we are to follow.

"Now when they heard this, they were pricked in their heart, and said unto Peter and to the rest of the apostles, 'Men and brethren,

what shall we do?' Then Peter said unto them, 'Repent, and be baptized every one of you in the name of Jesus Christ for the remission of sins, and ye shall receive the gift of the Holy Ghost.'" (Acts 2:37-38)

Repentance is the first stone we must lay in the foundation of a premier church. It is the action we immediately perform upon the recognition of our need for salvation. As Hebrews 6:1 declares, we are to, *". . . go on unto perfection; not laying again the foundation of repentance from dead works."* The doctrines of Christ listed in the next two verses are written in a very precise and important sequence. Salvation is listed first showing that we must have the first stone laid before we can move on to the second one, then the third, and so forth.

When we read, *"let us go on . . . not laying again,"* it implies that ultimately something must be built upon the foundation. But before something can be built, the foundation must be carefully laid with each stone in place.

If we were to build a house in the natural, one of the worst jobs we might face would be trying to rework the foundation after the house has been finished. It would be very difficult to correct.

The same thing is true in our Christian walk. I sincerely believe that most of the problems in the Christian church today exist because God's complete foundation has not been laid carefully and properly. Specifically, we have not understood the importance of repentance as the first foundation stone. As a result, we have some very serious and obvious weaknesses.

This brings to mind a story from the days of the Great Depression. In those days money was very scarce. Due to a lack of funds, a certain person neglected the care of his teeth. Inevitably he had a toothache and he decided he had better take care of it. He began to look through the Yellow Pages in search of the best deal when he spotted an advertisement for a painless dentist at a very reasonable price. He thought, *If I have to go and get my teeth taken care of anyway, I am going to go to a painless dentist.* So he went, and sure enough, he experienced almost no pain as the painless dentist fixed his teeth. He thanked the dentist wholeheartedly, paid his money, and left.

Six months later those very same teeth began to hurt again. He suspected that something had gone wrong with the other dentist so he made an appointment with a different one this time. When he arrived for his appointment he said to the new dentist, "I have had some work done on my teeth but my teeth are hurting." And the new dentist said, "I know who you've been to. You've been to the painless dentist!" "How did you know?" "Well, it's quite obvious. He did not remove all the decay, he just took off the surface of the decay, left the rest of it there, and filled over it. Now it is going to be much worse than if you'd had it done right in the beginning."

Christians today are often plagued with problems that should have been handled at the Cross. Our preoccupation with psychology, "inner healing," and all the other current popular therapies is caused by problems and sins that should have been handled at the Cross, but were not. The reason they were not is because people seek a painless religious experience, only to discover that the work of conversion was not totally done. Sin was not totally rooted out through the work of repentance. These new Christians still harbor bitterness and resentment, refuse to forgive others who have sinned against them, and cannot see anything wrong with some kinds of sin.

I am not in any way minimizing the importance of counseling. I am talking about believers who seem to always be in need of propping up. No matter how much counsel and pastoral care they get, they are still weak and unstable. Perhaps it is time for us to examine their foundation. Has the foundation of the doctrines of Christ been completely laid in their life? Have they laid a strong foundation of repentance?

Repentance, faith, baptism, and the gift of the Holy Spirit form the foundation of our spiritual lives. With that foundation in place we are then able to build well. We should not have to keep going back and reworking the foundation, making sure that all our sins are confessed and the skeletons in our closet are removed. We should not have to always be searching our foundation for cracks if it was laid properly in the first place.

The first, and perhaps most important, stone in our foundation is that of repentance. That is where everything begins in our Christian life. "Repent" was the theme of the Old Testament prophets. *"Repent, and turn yourselves from all your transgressions; so iniquity shall not be your ruin"* (Ezekiel 18:30). "Repent" is the first word of the Gospel. "Repent" was the first word in the message of John the Baptist. *"In those days came John the Baptist, preaching in the wilderness of Judea, and saying, 'Repent ye: for the kingdom of heaven is at hand'"* (Matthew 3:1-2). "Repent" was the first word in the message of Jesus. *"From that time Jesus began to preach, and to say, 'Repent: for the kingdom of heaven is at hand'"* (Matthew 4:17).

We have already seen that "Repent" was the first word of the message of the early church apostles. Paul's message was "Repent!" *"And the times of this ignorance God winked at; but now commandeth all men every where to repent"* (Acts 17:30). In fact, the word "repent(ance)" is used about sixty times in the New Testament. Repentance is where we must start in laying our foundation. If we do not understand repentance, or if we have a loose, sloppy attitude toward repentance, if we are seeking an easy, painless approach to the Gospel and our service of Christ, our Christian lives will be weak and unstable.

Our foundation must be built according to the pattern of God's Word. We cannot find redemption through the church. Redemption comes through the Cross and the process of the Cross. It is after redemption that the church finds its proper place in our lives. Until then, participation in the church is no substitute for repentance. And yet there are millions of people who go to church at all the right times and conclude that they are Christians. When they find themselves in church on Sunday or on Easter or on Christmas they think, *Look at me I am in church. After all, I am not a heathen, I am a Christian.* But that is no sign that they have laid the foundation of repentance in their experience. Without it, no matter how often they go to church and no matter how many good deeds they perform, they are not truly a follower of Jesus Christ.

The Greek transliteration for repentance is *metanoia.* It means to have a change of mind, or literally, to have another mind. Charles Finney defined repentance this way: "Changing your mind from what you have believed on any given subject to what God has revealed on that subject." For true believers in Christ, repentance is not something that just happens once.

Repentance is actually a spirit or an attitude of mind that we are to walk in all the time. In the book of Revelation, when Jesus sent certain letters to the seven churches in Asia through the Apostle John, He told the believers, not the unbelievers, to repent. Jesus was speaking to the churches in Asia. They had left their first love. Now they had to change their mind and go back to the Lord as at the first.

Repentance is not something that happens once. There is an initial experience of repentance that brings us into the kingdom of God, but the spirit of repentance is to then be in us all of the time. It is the spirit of repentance that motivates us to listen for the voice of the Lord. If He has something to say to us, we want to hear it. If what He says to us is contrary to our mindset, then we need to repent, turn from the way we have been thinking, change our minds, and allow the mind of Christ to be formed in us.

Repentance is not necessarily an emotion. It means that when we hear God's Word and discover that our thinking has been contrary to

His word, we repent. When we find out what God's revealed truth is on any subject, we need to repent and change our mind to conform to God's mind. That is repentance!

Let us discuss more fully what repentance is not:

1. Repentance Is Not the Conviction of Sin.

Conviction is not repentance, but rather leads to repentance. Feelings of guilt are not repentance. There are many people that come to the altar because they feel convicted of their sins. They do not necessarily feel the need to change, they just feel convicted and err if they assume that expressing their feelings of guilt equals repentance.

Godly sorrow may precede repentance. That is what happened in Acts 2:37 when the Holy Spirit caused the listeners in Jerusalem to be *"pricked in their heart."* They were convicted of their sin, but they had not yet repented. Unless there is a change in their thinking about the sin that results in an altered life, there is not true repentance.

2. Repentance Is Not Remorse.

Many people are convinced that remorse is the same as repentance. It is like the criminal who is really sorry, not for breaking the law, but for the penalty for breaking the law. He is not sorry that he is a sinner. He is sorry he got caught! He may stand before the judge and say with tears in his eyes, "I'm sorry." What he is really saying is, "I don't want to go to jail." He may really weep and hang his head. He may even convince the judge and jury that he ought to receive a light sentence. But that does not necessarily mean that he has repented. That is why so many convicts get out of jail and go right back to their life of crime.

In a church service or an evangelistic crusade, people will often feel the conviction of sin, the guilt for their transgressions, and maybe even sense the penalty of their sin—separation from God. As a result, they may respond to an altar call, and we will say, "Praise God, they just wept their way through to salvation." And then when we do not ever see them again, we wonder what happened to them. They cried, they said the "sinner's prayer," and now they have "backslidden." Why? Perhaps they, and we, did not give enough careful consideration to the need for true repentance. We thought of repentance as remorse. The guilt and pressure of the disaster brought upon them as a result of their sin produced a response of remorse. And so we are sometimes too quick to say, "Hallelujah, they got saved!" But if there is no change in their mindset, attitudes, thought patterns, and values; if they do not turn from their sins and self-centered ways to God, His will, and His ways, they have not repented. Tears often will accompany repentance, depending on the emotional makeup of the person. But a manifestation of remorse is not in itself proof of repentance.

3. Repentance Is Not Reformation.

Repentance is not just a determination to do better. It is not "turning over a new leaf" or a self-help program.

Repentance certainly does involve reformation. If we truly repent, we will turn around and start over in some very demonstrable ways. However, if God is not involved in the reformation, if it is not based on the work of the Cross, then it is not repentance and ultimately will fail.

Many people have a tradition of making New Year's resolutions. The beginning of a New Year is an excellent time to make a fresh start. But often it is only a matter of time until we have returned to our former way of life. The reason is simple: God was not at the center of the process. We were trying to change our flesh with our strength, and that never works. In fact, such will-centered efforts at personal reformation are the very dead works from which we are to repent. True repentance leads to faith toward God. In other words, it is God-centered.

4. Repentance Is Not Just Being Religious.

It is a common response to think that repentance leads to religious living. We master the religious jargon, pose, and tone of voice. People will then think we have repented.

The people that irritated Jesus the most were the Scribes and Pharisees–the religious people of that day! They were religion personified, but that did not impress the Lord. In fact, He ended up telling them that they had no part in the kingdom of God. He told them that they were worse than the completely irreligious people in society because not only did they refuse to enter into God's kingdom, they worked to keep others from doing so as well.

It is possible to attend a dynamic local church, learn all the praise choruses, raise our hands, shout "Hallelujah," serve in the church, go through all the motions, and still not repent.

5. Repentance Is Not "Only Believism."

Repentance involves more than an experience that takes place in the soul–it must touch our spirit. It is much more than a mental attitude. It is more than accepting the truth about Jesus and His kingdom. True repentance will always include a transformation of the whole life of the one who has repented–affecting the soul and the spirit.

Repentance is the most foundational truth in the Bible. Our walk with the Lord depends on our understanding and experience of it. Let's continue to ask the Lord to reveal to us not only what repentance is but also what it is not.

THE BASIS FOR REPENTANCE

Repentance is necessary because we have sinned. But what is the heart of sin? There are approximately 103 sins defined in the Bible in every category imaginable. But the root of each of those 103 rotten fruit is the same. The rejection of God, His Word, His rules, and His ways, all manifested through unbelief, is the root of sin. It is that root that must be dealt with through repentance.

Repentance is not ultimately focused on the specific sin but on the root. If we are going to truly and fully repent, we must be more than just sorry for our sin. Our repentance must be focused on the condition of our heart before a holy God.

It was Jeremiah who said, *"The heart is deceitful above all things, and desperately wicked: who can know it?"* (17:9). Isaiah gave the principle this way: *"All we like sheep have gone astray; we have turned every one to his own way"* (53:6). A person who has not repented is simply committed to going his own way and doing his own thing apart from God.

A person who has repented has experienced a transformation of his mind, thought patterns, and values. His mind has been changed so that it is in agreement with God in all that He has said. Formerly he had his own opinion, a different opinion from God's on every subject. When he has turned from himself and his sinful life to God, his thoughts change. He is no longer committed to going his own way. He is a Christian in that he is "Christ-like" and therefore "Word-like." His thoughts are being directed by the Holy Spirit and he has repented.

True repentance is based on the following:

1. A Recognition That We Have Sinned.

Those that Peter preached to on the day of Pentecost were "law-keepers." They were followers of Moses and keepers of the Judaism of their day. But the root of their sin was the fact that they had rejected Jesus as the Christ. They devoted their lives to studying the Old Testament, but when He came, they rejected the One who was the fulfillment of the Old Testament. When Peter preached the Gospel to them and they realized that they had rejected the Messiah, they knew that they had rejected God, His God's law, and were therefore separated from God. It is no wonder they said, "Now what are we going to do?" Upon that real-ization, Peter responded by calling them to repent.

2. A Recognition That We Are Responsible to Turn from Our Sins to God.

It is true that we cannot repent apart from the convicting work of the Holy Spirit. The Holy Spirit convicts as the Gospel is preached. The root sin of unbelief must be forsaken as a result of the conviction of the Holy Spirit. That is why Paul said, *"For whosoever shall call upon the name of the Lord shall be saved. How then shall they call on him in whom they have not believed? And how shall they believe in him of whom they have not heard? And how shall they hear without a preacher? So then faith cometh by hearing, and hearing by the word of God"* (Romans 10:13,14,17). Then after agreeing with the Gospel and trusting Christ for salvation, a new believer begins to live a life of simple obedience, beginning with obedience to the command of Christ to be baptized. That obedience is the fruit of repentance, it is the outward appearance of an inward work.

At first, it is the responsibility of the one who hears the Gospel and experiences the conviction of the Holy Spirit to respond with repen-tance. God has given everybody the ability to turn to Christ and believe. *"God hath dealt to every man the measure of faith"* (Romans 12:3). There is not a man on the face of this earth who does not have the God-given ability to turn to God and repent. It is the Holy Spirit who draws and convicts, but after He has done His work, the one being convicted must then decide whether or not he wants to repent. There must be an active choice to agree with God and accept His truth and authority.

It is the supernatural power of God that has been placed in the Gospel that enables each one to repent. It is that same power that enables the new believer to walk in the light of the Gospel. Conviction leads to conversion. But the step in between these two miracles of God's grace is our repentance.

Conviction is a miraculous work of the Holy Spirit. Conversion is miraculous. Repentance is a human responsibility. It is up to us. We are the ones who must admit that we are wrong and not walking in God's way. We must choose to walk with God. At that moment, Jesus Christ will come and forgive all our sins and cleanse us. He will then put a new heart in us and begin to lead us into an entirely new life. We will immediately sense the supernatural transformation that has taken place within us. We have all heard people testify that after they were born again the flowers seemed to be more beautiful, the air seemed fresher, things just looked different. Why? Because they had been converted. Their genuine repentance in response to the Gospel and the conviction of the Holy Spirit had forever changed their lives.

THE NEED FOR REPENTANCE

Repentance is mentioned sixty times in the Bible. If I stood before you and said something sixty times, would you conclude that it was important to me? At the same time, if God said something sixty times, would not you conclude that it was important to Him? The Lord has spoken the word of repentance to us sixty times. It is important to Him that we understand repentance. If it is impossible to be birthed into the kingdom of God unless we choose to turn toward God, then repentance is vitally important to each one of us.

Here are seven reasons why we must repent:

1. God Commands Us to Repent.

His commandment is immediate and universal. *"And the times of this ignorance God winked at; but now commandeth all men every where to repent"* (Acts 17:30). Repentance is not an option, it is a universal demand from the Creator. He is saying, "If you want My help in your life, if you want Me to forgive and cleanse you, walk with you, help and give you purpose and direction in life, as well as eternal life to come, then you must come to me through repentance." There are no exceptions. He commanded all men everywhere to repent.

2. Repentance Was the Reason Christ Came into the World.

"I came not to call the righteous, but sinners to repentance" (Luke 5:32).

Why did Jesus come? He came to call the sinner to repentance. As a result, everyone will be judged by his or her response to the call of Jesus. There is no other righteousness but the one Jesus has given. If a person does not sense a genuine need for God, does not see the need to walk in His ways, and has no desire to repent, then the Lord simply cannot help him!

Jesus came for the sinner. He came for the one who senses his need for the grace of God. Jesus came for the purpose of calling that one back to Himself, and giving him an opportunity of being reconciled with God. When the repentant sinner turns to Christ, he meets Jesus at the foot of the cross and his life is forever changed.

3. Repentance is Necessary to Avoid Destruction.

"I tell you, Nay: but, except ye repent, ye shall all likewise perish" (Luke 13:3,5).

We may be sincere and morally good people, but if we are not in full agreement with God's truth—not relying on Christ alone for salvation and righteousness—then we are sinners and will bear the consequences. Christ is calling us to repent so that we will not perish.

4. Repentance is Necessary for Forgiveness.

"Repent ye therefore, and be converted, that your sins may be blotted out" (Acts 3:19).

"If thy brother trespass against thee, rebuke him; and if he repent, forgive him" (Luke 17:3).

Notice the sequence—first repentance, then forgiveness. God cannot forgive unrepentant people. We cannot be released from our sins and the penalty of those sins unless we consciously seek forgiveness through repentance.

Forgiveness is a principle of the universe. Forgiveness is how you and I became Christians. But we were not forgiven until we had repented. No one is forgiven without repentance. If someone comes to the Lord Jesus and says, "I want to be a Christian, I want to go to heaven," the Lord responds by saying, "Wonderful! I am inviting you to be with me forever!" So they say, "Okay, I accept Jesus. I want to go to heaven. I am in, am I not? I believe in Jesus." Not necessarily! Not until you have fully repented. He must change his mind, agree with the Bible, and obey God's Word concerning every area of life. When we say, "God, I have sinned against You and I am turning to You," and mean it sincerely, then He will forgive you.

5. Repentance Is Necessary for Entrance into the Kingdom of God.

"Repent: for the kingdom of heaven is at hand" (Matthew 4:17).

The kingdom of God is within our reach. But there is no way we can be "born again" except that we repent. And the only way to gain entrance into the kingdom of God is by being "born again." *"Verily, verily, I say unto thee, Except a man be born again, he cannot see the king-*

dom of God" (John 3:3). There is no way we can be delivered out of the kingdom of darkness and translated into the kingdom of His dear Son unless we repent (see Colossians 1:13). There is no way we can be cleansed from our sins unless we repent. There is no way we can avoid the destruction that faces our life unless we repent.

6. Repentance Is God's Desire for All Men.

"The Lord is not slack concerning his promise, as some men count slackness; but is longsuffering to us-ward, not willing that any should perish, but that all should come to repentance" (2 Peter 3:9).

It is the great desire and longing of the heart of our God that all men everywhere repent and turn to Him to receive His life. God so loved the world that He gave everything heaven could offer so men would repent and receive Him and His life.

7. Repentance Leads to Life.

"When they heard these things, they held their peace, and glorified God, saying, 'Then hath God also to the Gentiles granted repentance unto life'" (Acts 11:18).

Repentance does not lead to bondage. When we repent and turn to Jesus, He gives us true life. Some people say, "If I come to Jesus and make Him the Lord of my life I will not be able to do fun things any more and I'll have to do all these boring, weird things until Jesus comes." That is not the right way to look at it. The Bible says that a full life comes from serving the Lord. He alone can give us life. It is repentance that leads to life.

This is the Bible pattern: conviction, repentance, conversion, and life! If you are not enjoying your walk with Jesus Christ, go back to the altar. Get another dentist! Repent! Turn your mind away from all ungodliness, reject the desire to live for yourself, change your mind, and agree with God's Word. In short, repent!

PRINCIPLES OF REPENTANCE

The Lord has spoken to us about the need to carefully lay a spiritual foundation for our life. The place where we must begin is the foundation stone of repentance. We have seen the nature of repentance and the basis for repentance. Now we will look at some clear, simple Bible principles regarding our experience of repentance. Here are four words that are connected to repentance in the Scriptures:

1. The Will

In His letter to the church in Thyatira found in Revelation 2:20-22, Jesus referred to the need of that church to judge Jezebel. She did not repent for her fornication when God gave her an opportunity to do so and Jesus wrote that He would judge her for it. Jezebel chose with her will not to repent. Repentance is an act of our will.

It is true that if the Holy Spirit does not convict us, we cannot repent. That is why we cannot say, "Well, I am going to have a few more flings, I am going to sow some more wild oats, I am going to wait until I am a little older, and then I'll settle down and get a little religion." It just does not work that way. We are not in control of when we will repent. We must repent when God convicts us. We cannot draw ourselves to God, He draws us.

2. Faith

The words "repentance" and "faith" are often found together in the Bible. *"Testifying both to the Jews, and also to the Greeks, repentance toward God, and faith toward our Lord Jesus Christ"* (Acts 20:21). Faith is always involved with repentance. When we repent and turn our mind away from the evil of our soul and our past, we do it so that we can become connected with God. We repent so that we can now believe. Jesus Christ calls us to repentance because he wants us to place our faith in Him, come to know Him, and receive His life. That is faith, and is to always follow repentance.

3. Baptism

Repentance leads to baptism. It is the next step for the believer who has truly repented. *"Then Peter said unto them, 'Repent, and be baptized every one of you in the name of Jesus Christ for the remission of sins, and ye shall receive the gift of the Holy Ghost'"* (Acts 2:38). The initial sign that we have repented and believed in Jesus for salvation is baptism. There is more to water baptism than that, but the point is that baptism reveals our obedient attitude toward Christ and His Word. It shows that we have repented.

4. Conversion

When combined together, the principles of the will, faith, and baptism result in this final principle—the principle of conversion. *"Repent ye therefore, and be converted, that your sins may be blotted out, when the times of refreshing shall come from the presence of the Lord"* (Acts 3:19). It is not that we should repent and then return to our former way of life. The command is, "Repent, and be converted." Conversion implies change—practical, demonstrable change in the details of our lives. It means that when we repent and turn to Christ, we change the entire direction of our lives. All the old things pass away and everything becomes new. We have new desires, standards, goals, and values—everything is new!

Clearly the foundation of repentance is of ultimate importance to our lives. Our conversion and ongoing walk with the Lord depends on it. The truth of repentance must be central in our minds as we share the Gospel with others.

But more than that, the principle of repentance is the key to our spiritual growth. Our constant responsiveness to the voice of the Lord determines the progress of our walk with the Lord. It is as we allow the Word of God to adjust us that we will grow more and more into the image of Christ.

God has commanded everyone, everywhere to repent. Repentance is the reason the Lord Jesus Christ came into the world. It is necessary to avoid destruction. It is necessary for forgiveness. Repentance provides entry into the kingdom of God. Repentance is God's desire for everyone. God is saying that He wants us to turn around and believe what He said in His Word.

This principle of repentance is the fundamental truth upon which we must build our Christian lives. This is the fundamental truth upon which all congregations must lay their foundation.

CHAPTER SIX

Preserving Truth:
The Fear of God

REQUIREMENTS

We are living in an age when we see very little respect for authority or fear of the Lord—and for the same reason. If we do not teach respect for authority in the local church, there will be a corresponding lack of respect for God.

This can also apply to the home. If children are not taught to respect mom and dad, to that degree they are also not going to respect God and His authority outside of the home. In other words, disrespect for authority is the worst thing parents or pastors could allow to continue.

A strong disregard for authority is the general condition of our society today. Because of that, there is a great lack of people who live in the fear of God. The fear of God, a healthy respect for His sovereign rule in our lives, always begins with respect for authority in general. As people grow to respect natural authority and come into an understanding of their Father God, they will automatically respect Him as well. But if they do not respect authority in the home or in the House of God, it is going to be hard to teach them the fear of God. Being able to teach the fear of the Lord is vitally important to the success and fruitfulness of the church. Here is the principle I want you to see: No single aspect of the Christian walk carries with it greater promises of blessing than to walk in the fear of the Lord.

It is no wonder Satan is seeking to destroy the fear of God in the church. We are always talking about the promises of God, the blessings of God, prosperity, etc, but we rarely hear about the fear of God. This is tragic because all of the blessings we talk about are connected with and dependent upon living in the fear of God.

An incident took place in my life at the age of 16 that clearly illustrates the importance of teaching the fear of God and respect for authority. In fact, this event was probably a crossroad in my life. If it had not turned out as it did, I do not think that I would be serving the Lord as I am now.

I was a normal sixteen-year-old raised in a Christian home. Both my dad and mom loved the Lord and they raised me in the house of God. But when I reached my teen years, I decided I would test Dad's authority to see just how far I could push him. As often happens at that age, I was having some tension in my relationship with my dad. He was a man of strong convictions. He was a short Norwegian man of forty-six, and at sixteen, I was taller than him. He also was a physically strong man, having been a mechanic with his own garage before becoming a pastor. He was strong, but I thought I was pretty big stuff too!

Dad had been on my back telling me, "No, you cannot do this," and "No, you cannot do that," and "you will do this," and "you will do that!" I began to react. I respected him, but the exercise of his authority was starting to get in the way of my desires. One night in our living room he told me I could not do something I wanted to do, and with eyes glaring I said to him, "I am going to do it anyway, Dad." Now normally I would have ducked! But this time I stood my ground. He looked me straight in the eye and said, "Son, you are not going to do it!" Then I began to argue with him until he said, "You just keep your mouth shut and do what I told you to do!" I stood there with my fist clinched. Then I lost my cool and said, "I've had it! I'm leaving this house!"

I then turned and walked over to the front door of the house, opened it, walked out, slammed the door behind me, and began to head down the street. I was determined that I was not going to hang around my father's house any longer. To this day I cannot believe that I ever did that. You just did not mouth off to my dad because he believed in "child abuse!" But I was on my way. I was going to go down that street, hitch a ride to California and get out of that bondage!

I was stubborn and full of rebellion and was heading across the yard toward the street when my dad reached the front door. All he said was, "Young man, get back in here now!" Without pausing, I stopped in my tracks, turned around, and walked back into the house. There is no question that what stopped me was the fear of my father. If I had not had that kind of respect for my father, I would have taken off, hitch-hiked to California, and gotten involved in sin. What kept me was the fact that I feared him. When his voice said, "Young man, you get back in here now!" something he had put in me as a child triggered a response. Even in the midst of a spirit of rebellion, the fear of my dad determined my actions. And I thank God for that!

The fear of God is a tool that the Lord can use in our lives when everything else fails. In the early days of the church, the people walked in it. After Peter preached the Gospel to those who had gathered on the day of Pentecost, Acts 2:43 states that *"Fear came upon every soul."* A good, healthy respect for God was clearly evident in the church.

Fear is not torment, but a holy reverence for God. Notice that fear came upon every soul. In other words, of the 3,120 members in this church, every one of them feared God.

This continued to be the pattern in the early church. *"And great fear came upon all the church"* (Acts 5:11). Acts 9:31 states that all the churches throughout Judea, Galilee, and Samaria walked in the fear of the Lord.

A Gallop poll on religion in America was released several years ago. According to the poll there were approximately fifty million Americans who claimed to be "born-again." When I first read that I thought, *Wow, there is a real revival going on! Almost one out of five Americans are born-again Christians!* But then the poll went on to report that when asked the question, "Has your experience of being born again affected your lifestyle?" only 12 percent said that it had. That means 88 percent of those claiming to be "born again" did not consider it relevant to their lifestyle. They just continued on with their lives and added Jesus to their religious experience without it resulting in any practical difference at all.

Here is a simple definition of the fear of God: An awesome reverence and respect towards God, knowing that He is totally righteous and full of mercy and truth, compensating and rewarding the obedient in faith, and to the contrary, judging, chastening, and punishing the disobedient in faith.

This is a definition each of us needs to carefully ponder. Satan would like to destroy the fear of God in the hearts of God's people and in the heart of the church. The reason is simple: if a believer does not fear God (in a healthy way), he will not be a fruitful Christian. Instead, he will tend to think of God as a kind of Santa Claus—just a jolly old fellow out to do nothing but bless him. For this kind of God, anything goes. But a healthy fear of God, as I have defined it above, will alone result in the blessings of God being poured out upon the believer.

If the fear of the Lord is so important, why do we often shirk from the very term? Here are some reasons:

1. Because We Often Associate the Fear of God, and Even the Term "Fear," with Natural Fear.

We have certain natural fears that are good because they keep us from doing foolish things. We may experience fear when we are on a high mountain or in some other dangerous situation. This kind of fear is designed for our preservation. We are not talking about natural fear when we are talking about the fear of God.

2. Because Some People Think of Fear Only in the Sense of Demonic Fear.

The Bible says that, *"God hath not given us the spirit of fear"* (2 Timothy 1:7). It also says that *"fear hath torment"* (1 John 4:18). There are all sorts of fears of this kind—claustrophobia, fear of heights, fear of darkness, fear of crowds, etc. These are often demonic fears. This is not the fear of the Lord. *"For ye have not received the spirit of bondage again to fear"* (Romans 8:15).

3. Because Some People Mistake Purely Religious Fear with the Fear of the Lord.

"Forasmuch as this people draw near me with their mouth, and with their lips do honour me, but have removed their heart far from me, and their fear toward me is taught by the precept of men." (Isaiah 29:13)

Religious fear is the result of being involved in a religious, legalistic lifestyle. Because of religious fear we often shirk back from the true fear of God.

4. Because Others Mistake the Fear of Man for the Fear of the Lord.

"The fear of man bringeth a snare" (Proverbs 29:25)

There are many people who fear man and think that they fear of God. They allow the faces of men to cause them to withdraw and they lose their confidence in the Lord. This is not what we mean by the fear of God.

Our misconceptions of the fear of God cause many to not walk in it. I love to speak on the love of God, His grace, and the unmerited favor He shows us. But twice as much is said in the Scriptures about the fear of God as the love of God, making it important that we teach on that as well.

I was raised in a very legalistic church. I remember a Sunday school lesson I was taught when I was about 8 or 9 years old. The teacher was a lady dressed in black with her hair in a bun. For forty-five minutes, she taught us from a Scripture in Proverbs about the person who *"win-keth with the eye"* (10:10). She went on and on telling us that if we wink, we are sinning. To this day, every time I wink, I experience a pang of guilt. She got her message across!

That is the kind of teaching I had while growing up. I remember thinking that if I had a bad thought as Jesus was returning, I would go to hell forever. I lived in a state of bondage as a young person. I would try desperately to have one day, just one day, where I did not blow it (where I did not wink)! And I watched the group of young people I grew up with finally give up and begin a life of sin.

When I talk about the fear of God, I am not talking about some kind of religious, legalistic attitude toward God. He is not a big giant in the sky with a club just waiting for us to make a mistake so that he can squash us like a bug. But neither is he a wimpy little fellow patting us on the head, saying, "I don't care if you disobey me. You just do what-ever you want. It doesn't matter." God is totally righteous and faithful to enforce His laws of righteousness.

When I was very young, my dad got a message through to me very clearly—disobedience resulted in pain. As I continued to grow, disobedi-ence consistently produced pain. On the other hand, obedience pro-duced blessings. When I made a commitment to my heavenly Father, that principle was a part of my commitment. I automatically knew that obedience would bring blessings while disobedience would bring pain. My walk with the heavenly Father worked the same way as it had with my earthly dad. If I did not do what God told me to do, He disciplined me. I got that message when I was young in my Christian life. As a result, I have never walked away from the Lord to pursue a life of sin. I have disobeyed, I have sinned, but I have never gone back on my basic commitment to the Lord. Because I was taught a healthy fear of my father, when I made my own commitment to Jesus Christ as my Lord and God, it was very easy for me to understand that God was going to enforce obedience. He is righteous and cannot walk away from disobedience without administering correction.

When my first child, Debi, was about two years old, I had a very interesting experience with her. One evening, it was my turn to baby-sit. It was really my first occasion to take care of her alone. As she was toddling around the room I said to her, "Debi, come here." When she heard her name she looked back at me and then proceeded to wander off. So I said it again, "Debi, come here." She looked at me again and then just toddled off. So I got up and took hold of her and led her over to me. I did not raise my voice, but just brought her over to the couch and we played together for a little while. After a while I let her walk away and then I said again, "Debi, come here." She just toddled off. I said it twice, clearly, and then I got up and brought her to me, only a little more firmly. "Daddy said, 'Come here.'" Then she began to sense that something was wrong. I never raised my voice, I just persisted in this way maybe fifteen times. The Scriptures tell us to *"train up a child"* (Proverbs 22:6). The word "train" means "to teach by repetition." So I just continued to repeat the lesson.

Finally tears began to come when I brought her over to me. She knew something was wrong and that Dad was upset with her. Finally, I said, "Debi, come here," a great big smile just burst on her face. She had learned her lesson. She walked right over to me and then we played together for a while. For several hours she would wander off, almost waiting for me to say, "Debi, come here," so I would play with her. The discipline became a fun little game.

I never thought too much about it, but I put something in her that night. It took a couple of hours one evening, but from that time on whenever I would say, "Debi, come here," she would come. I did this with the other three children after that, and I saw how easy it was to put some of these basic principles into them when they are young. Later when the kids were teenagers, I would go into a big youth gathering where everybody was screaming and laughing, and say just loudly enough so she could hear me, "Debi, come here," and in the middle of the noise she would hear her father's voice and respond.

I use that illustration, not because I think I am such a good father, but because of the principle involved. If my daughter respects her father, it is going to be easier for her to respect the Lord. I thank the Lord that all of our children are serving the Lord—they learned to fear their dad and that helped them learn to fear the Lord.

Solomon was known as the wisest man on earth. At the end of his life his conclusion was this, *"Let us hear the conclusion of the whole matter: Fear God, and keep his commandments: for this is the whole duty of man"* (Ecclesiastes 12:13). That summarized it for Solomon. Why? *"For God shall bring every work into judgment, with every secret thing, whether it be good, or whether it be evil"* (v. 14). Not some, but every work. Every secret thing, whether it be good or whether it be evil, will be judged by a righteous God in the end. A fear of the Lord will help us perform works that will be judged as good.

There is a principle to learn from this: Whatever we fear the most, we will worship. If we fear nothing, we worship ourselves. There are those that do not fear God or man. They worship themselves—the creature rather than the Creator. Since they do not fear God, they do not worship Him. We cannot be a worshiper of God if we do not fear Him. David said of worship, *"unite my heart to fear thy name"* (Psalm 86:11). In other words, do not let me come with a heart that lacks respect.

"Who shall ascend into the hill of the Lord? Or who shall stand in his holy place? He that hath clean hands, and a pure heart" (Psalm 24:3-4). If we come before Him without clean hands and a pure heart, it shows a lack of the fear of the Lord. We must come to Him with reverence and honor for His great and holy name. True worship is communion with the Lord that grows out of a deep love and respect for God, knowing that He is totally righteous, loves us, and will bless us if we diligently seek Him. But true worship is also based on a conviction that the Lord is sovereign and will punish the disobedient. We must come before the Lord in worship with a focus on His greatness. We must not worship Him with a casual attitude. He is not our pal! He is the Almighty Creator of the universe, my Lord and God, and my heavenly Father.

This was certainly true of our Lord Jesus.

"And there shall come forth a rod out of the stem of Jesse, and a Branch shall grow out of his roots: And the spirit of the Lord shall rest upon him, the spirit of wisdom and understanding, the spirit of counsel and might, the spirit of knowledge and of the fear of the Lord." (Isaiah 11:1-2)

Of the sevenfold nature of the Spirit of the Lord that rested on Christ, the last aspect was the Spirit "of the fear of the Lord." One of the chief characteristics of Christ was that He feared God. He respected and had reverence for His heavenly Father. This factor is emphasized twice in this prophecy. Not only shall the Messiah be given the Spirit of the fear of the Lord, but that same Spirit *"shall make him of quick under-standing in the fear of the Lord"* (Isaiah 11:3).

This is evident through a study of the life of Christ. Jesus claimed that *"The Son can do nothing of himself, but what he seeth the Father do: for what things soever he doeth, these also doeth the Son likewise"* (John

5:19). Jesus only said what the Father told Him to say. He only did what the Father told Him to do. He only went where the Father told Him to go. He was an example of complete and consistent obedience to the Father. Why was He able to live that way? He was filled with the Spirit of the fear of the Lord. He had a quick understanding of the fear of God. His quick response to the Father was one of obedience that was the result of respect, reverence, and a sense of dependence on His Father. His constant attitude was, *"not my will, but thine, be done"* (Luke 22:42), and *"My meat is to do the will of him that sent me, and to finish his work"* (John 4:34). That attitude was the clearest demonstration that He was a man who feared the Lord.

In our desire to see the blessings of God come to us and the promises of God fulfilled in our lives, we must be very careful to make sure that we are not at the center of our lives, our goals, and our desires. When the focus of our faith and prayers is on "God bless me and give to me and meet my needs and be nice to me, me, me, me, me," we know that our primary concern is not for God's honor and glory but for our own benefit. To that degree we are not living in the fear of the Lord! That does not mean that God does not want to bless us. It means that only those who fear the Lord and put Him first really experience the blessings of the Lord.

Let us carefully consider a final passage of Scripture:

> *"And if ye call on the Father, who without respect of persons judgeth according to every man's work, pass the time of your sojourning here in fear: Forasmuch as ye know that ye were not redeemed with corruptible things, as silver and gold, from your vain conversation received by tradition from your fathers; but with the precious blood of Christ, as of a lamb without blemish and without spot."* (1 Peter 1:17-19)

Peter gives us the two basic reasons why we should walk in the fear of God.

1. God Is Going to Judge Us According to What We Have Done in Our Bodies During Our Lives Here on Earth.

He is going to judge every man according to his work, without respect of persons. All disobedience will be judged in the end. On the other hand, all acts of obedience will result in the Lord's blessings.

2. Because of the Awesome Price that He Paid for Our Redemption.

We fear God because of the cross and all the implications of the tremendous work of the cross. We should never tire of speaking of the cross for that is the single most important act of obedience ever accomplished. It is the cross that brings an awesome reverence and respect for God. He redeemed us, not with corruptible things, but with the precious blood of Jesus.

BENEFITS OF THE FEAR OF THE LORD

So far we have seen the requirements of the fear of the Lord through the call of the Spirit in the church today and in the example of the early church. Let us review the blessings promised to us when we live our lives in the fear of the Lord. Remember, no single aspect of the Christian life carries with it greater promises of blessing than to the man who walks in the fear of the Lord.

1. The Promise of Wisdom

"Behold, the fear of the Lord, that is wisdom." (Job 28:28)

"The fear of the Lord is the beginning of wisdom: a good understanding have they that do his commandments." (Psalm 111:10)

There is a difference between education and wisdom. You can educate a fool, but that does not make him wise. *"The fool hath said in his heart, There is no God"* (Psalm 14:1). A man is only wise if he fears God. And he is a wise man because God is able to direct the steps of his life as a result of living his life in the fear of the Lord. It is impossible to have a response of obedience to the word of the Lord if we do not have the fear of the Lord. For instance, *"Christ [is] as a son over his own house; whose house are we, if we hold fast the confidence and the rejoicing of the hope firm unto the end"* (Hebrews 3:6). This is a conditional statement—its fulfillment is based on our response. If we hold fast to the word that is written to us, if we have an ear to hear what the Holy Spirit is saying to us, then the promise of the Lord will be fulfilled. The only person that has that kind of response is the one who fears God.

If we do not fear God we will say, "Well, I don't think that's so important, I'll just skip that. I don't think I have to be baptized. I don't think I really need to tithe. It's not that big of a deal. God understands." After a while we will begin to realize that we do not seem to have much wisdom. Things will seem to be falling apart. We will not be able to come up with any answers. We will say the wrong thing and make the wrong decisions most of the time, because we do not have a real fear of the Lord. Fearing God leads to wisdom for our lives.

2. The Promise of Spiritual Cleansing

"The fear of the Lord is clean, enduring forever." (Psalm 19:9)

The fear of the Lord is like a disinfectant. It will keep us morally and spiritually clean. If we do not fear God, we will tend to become defiled much more easily.

The fear of the Lord is not only clean, it endures forever. It will protect us from defilement. It will keep us from making the kind of mistakes we all tend to make when we are not walking in the fear of the Lord.

3. The Promise of Guidance, Instruction, and Prosperity

"What man is he that feareth the Lord? Him shall he teach in the way that he shall choose. His soul shall dwell at ease; and his seed shall inherit the earth. The secret of the Lord is with them that fear him; and he will shew them his covenant." (Psalm 25:12-14)

There is a lot said about prosperity today but it is never said in the context of the fear of God. This psalm offers true prosperity. Do we want to learn the secrets of God? Fear the Lord! He will come to us and share His heart with us. In the end we will inherit the earth. That will be true prosperity! Our problem is that we tend to make prosperity into an end in itself. It is the fear of the Lord we must seek. Then when the Lord blesses us, we will not make His blessings into gods.

The Lord wants to bless us. Jesus said that *"no man that hath left house, or brethren, or sisters, or father, or mother, or wife, or children, or lands, for my sake, and the gospel's, but he shall receive an hundredfold now in this time, houses, and brethren, and sisters, and mothers, and children, and lands, with persecutions; and in the world to come eternal life."* (Mark 10:29-30). But the blessings of the Lord are always connected to the fear of the Lord. We are not to seek the Lord's blessings out of self-interest. If we do, we serve the Lord out of ulterior motives, and if He does not give us the blessings we seek, we will not serve Him with all our hearts and lives. Instead, we are to seek the Lord in the fear of the Lord. In the end it is the meek, those who fear the Lord and walk in obedience to the Lord, who will inherit the earth. They will know true prosperity, and it will not destroy them. It will be a source of blessing to them and to all who are around them. It will be a blessing to the house of God because the ones being blessed are walking in the fear of the Lord, so they will know how to respond and what to do with the blessings the Lord gives them.

4. The Promise of Long Life

"The fear of the Lord prolongeth days: but the years of the wicked shall be shortened." (Proverbs 10:27)

Want a long, satisfying, fruitful life? Fear the Lord! The chastening that comes due to our folly and the lack of the fear of the Lord can involve or cause a shortening of our days. Disobedience can shorten our days on the earth. For example: *"He that eateth and drinketh unworthily, eateth and drinketh damnation to himself, not discerning the Lord's body. For this cause many are weak and sickly among you, and many sleep"* (1 Corinthians 11:29-30). In other words, where believers do not have the fear of God, they will tend to be careless in discerning the Lord's body. They will tend to not have an adequate appreciation for either the body of Christ on the cross or for the church as the body of Christ. As a result, they will gossip, tear each other down, and step all over the church. Paul is saying that when that happens, the length of their days and the degree of their fruitfulness will be cut short. The fear of God will keep us in love with the members of the body of Christ. The lack of the fear of God will result in disobedience and the pain of discipline. The fear of the Lord will result in a full life.

5. The Promise of Deliverance from All Other Kinds of Fear

There are many fears that torment us, but the fear of God will deliver us from all other kinds of fear. Because God is in control of our lives, if we fear God, he will deliver us from all other fears.

"In the fear of the Lord is strong confidence: and his children shall have a place of refuge. The fear of the Lord is a fountain of life, to depart from the snares of death." (Proverbs 14:26,27)

The fear of the Lord will enable us to depart from all other fears. It is the fountain of life. Other fears may harass us, but the fear of the Lord will deliver us from the snares of death and we will have strong confidence and a place of refuge.

6. The Promise of Abiding Satisfaction and Freedom from Evil

"The fear of the Lord tendeth to life: and he that hath it shall abide satisfied; he shall not be visited with evil" (Proverbs 19:23); or "The fear of the Lord leads to life; Then one rests content, untouched by trouble." (NIV)

That Scripture does not mean we will never have trouble. It means that we will not be scarred by trouble. God will give us the ability to go through our problems without them devastating our lives. Our lives will never be disturbed. The Lord will enable us to walk through trouble and not fear it. The fear of God will keep that trouble from touching us. It means that we will never lose the victory. Trouble will not defeat us if we have the fear of God.

Some years ago there was a beautiful young lady in our church who was in her back yard doing some work. Her husband was not home at the time. As she worked, a man stepped out of the bushes, grabbed her and drug her into her own house. There he tied her to a chair. She was helpless as he taped her mouth shut—she could not move or speak. He then ransacked the home and took all the valuables. After about 45 minutes he reappeared and he told her he was going to rape her. He took out his knife and he began to cut her clothes off her body. She was totally helpless so she began to pray in the Spirit. Only God could protect her now. As she was praying in the Spirit suddenly she sensed no movement in the room. She was still bound but the man had left. He had not raped her. He had started to cut off her clothes, but then for some reason he left.

She managed to free herself enough to get to the phone and dialed her husband at his office. I happened to be in his office when the call came. She was hysterical of course.

We hastily went to the home. Thank God she had not been raped or physically hurt, but this scripture came into my mind, *". . . [you] shall not be visited with evil"* (Proverbs 19:23). That simply means that though we go through trouble it does not have to scar us for the rest of our lives.

Normally speaking, this couple would want to move out of their house and all her life she would live in fear of this happening again. She might even need psychological treatment to experience inner healing. But as we prayed together in that home, I quoted her that scripture. She was a woman who feared God. She did not have to be scarred by this.

It is now years later and when I see her I ask if she has had any aftereffects from that terrible day. It is almost as though she does not know what I am talking about. Then she smiles and says, "No, I had a couple nightmares at first, but now I don't even think about it." They stayed in their home (they did put a big dog in the back yard!).

We will not be scarred by our tragedies.

7. Promise of a Secure Future

"By humility and the fear of the Lord are riches, and honour, and life." (Proverbs 22:4)

"Let not thine heart envy sinners: but be thou in the fear of the Lord all the day long. For surely there is an end; and thine expectation shall not be cut off." (Proverbs 23:17,18)

The fear of the Lord will bring us a secure future. When we exercise it in our lives, we will receive riches, honor, and life. God will grant us the ability to relax and enjoy the blessings we receive by living in the fear of the Lord.

Now that we know about the fear of God, what are we going to do about it? We need to make some practical applications of this important truth.

First, we need to realize that the fear of the Lord can be taught. *"Come . . . I will teach you the fear of the Lord"* (Psalm 34:11). The fear of the Lord is not primarily an emotion. It is a way of thinking and responding that can be taught. We are to simply explain to people that God is a God of righteousness. If they walk against His known will, He is going to chasten them because He cannot ignore disobedience. He would be a dishonest Father if He said that we would be chastened for disobedience and then did not chasten us. God wants us to learn how important obedience is to him. It is only as we learn to obey Him that He can guide our lives; and it is only as He directs our lives that He can bless us. That is why it is so important that we teach the fear of God.

The psalmist gives us a beautiful example of teaching the fear of the Lord:

"Give ear, O my people, to my law: incline your ears to the words of my mouth. I will open my mouth in a parable: I will utter dark sayings of old: which we have heard and known, and our fathers have told us. We will not hide them from their children, shewing to the generation to come the praises of the Lord, and his strength, and his wonderful works that he hath done. For he established a testimony in Jacob, and appointed a law in Israel, which he commanded our fathers, that they should make them known to their children: that the generation to come might know them, even the children which should be born; who should arise and declare them to their children: that they might set their hope in God, and not forget the works of God, but keep his commandments." (Psalm 78:1-7)

This principle applies to every one of us, starting in our homes. It is addressed to fathers concerning the instruction of children, whether they are natural or spiritual children. It must be applied in our homes and in the household of faith. I recommend that we have times when we review the dramatic, miraculous dealings of the Lord in the local church as well. No matter how many times the people hear it, it impresses upon them the might, power, and faithfulness of the Lord.

I remember my parents giving me this kind of instruction when I was a small boy. Mom would say, "Son, soon after you were born, you were not expected to live. You were born prematurely with a double hernia. After six weeks you weighed less than when you were born. The doctors said you were going to die. And you know what we did? We bundled you up and took you down to the little Assembly of God church where Dad and I found Jesus as Lord. You were just skin and bones, you were about dead, but we took you down and asked the pastor if he would anoint you with oil. And they put oil on your head and prayed for you and the Lord healed you! Miraculously! Without an operation, things came back into order in your little body. You started eating, and look at you now!" Mom and Dad would tell us continually of the wonderful works of God. And that put an awesome respect for God in our minds as children.

Each one of us has experienced the miraculous in our lives. God has intervened and touched us and healed us! Tell those stories to the children. Tell them over and over again. They love to hear about God's miraculous wonders! As a result, their hope will be established in God.

God wants us to fear the Lord, and He promises us that if we do, His blessings will rest upon us. Those who do not fear the Lord will know torment and not experience the Lord's blessings. It was a few years ago that this really dawned on me. I began to search the Scriptures and God showed me the tremendous blessings that are promised to those who fear the Lord. As a result, I responded in several ways, both personally and in the congregation. I began by asking the Lord to forgive me for my personal lack of the fear of the Lord and of minimizing its importance. Then I called on the congregation to seek forgiveness for their personal lack in this area. Finally, I made a clear commitment to walk in the fear of God. No longer did I want to become so accustomed to the ways of God that I would take them for granted. I always wanted to hold the Lord in awesome respect. I committed myself to keeping my will under God's will. I determined that whenever I had to make a decision, if I did not feel it was the Lord's will, no matter how difficult it was for me, I was not going to do it. I was going to seek first the kingdom of God and His righteousness, His will, His way, and only then would all His other blessings come to me.

I have often thought of how it must have been in the early church. How I desire to have the same awesome awareness of God's presence that they had. What if we had been there, had witnessed the resurrection of Christ, had seen His nail-printed hands, had personally heard Him say, "I am going to go away, but I will come back. But I am going to send you My Holy Spirit who will be My presence among you. And where two or three are gathered together, I am going to be there." Then to have gathered in that first church, knowing that Jesus was there. What a thrill it must have been. They had seen the resurrection, they had seen the ascension, they were filled with the Holy Spirit, they knew His word was true and so they knew Jesus was actually there with them. Imagine how excited they must have been!

What would happen if Jesus walked visibly into one of our gatherings? We would probably fall on our faces in worship! What we do not appreciate enough is the fact that He is here! The Lord wants us to have the same awareness of His presence today. If we do, our children also will have that awareness and soon learn to walk in the fear of the Lord. A healthy fear of the Lord protects us from all other fears.

CHAPTER SEVEN

Revering Truth:
The Sabbath Principle

Lately many vital old truths have begun to fade into the background of the church. One of these is the truth of the Lord's day, or the "Sabbath Principle."

As a pastor, I have observed that when someone begins to take the Lord's day lightly, spiritual decline is in his future. I am sure other pastors and Christian leaders have made the same observation. I believe that very time a believer takes the Lord's day lightly, he is headed for spiritual problems.

Why is that true? What does the Bible have to say about the Lord's day and why is it so important? Why do we still gather together on the Lord's day, even though we are in the new covenant era? Why not treat every day alike? Why not just do our own thing on the Lord's day and trust in the grace of God to cover us? What is the Sabbath Principle?

THE SABBATH PRINCIPLE AND FRUITFULNESS

Is there any link between being fruitful and honoring the Lord's day? The Lord has spoken to us about touching the world with the Gospel. It is clear that the Lord wants us to be fruitful. Is there some connection between the fruitfulness of our lives and the Sabbath Principle? When we talk about fruitfulness, we are not referring to material blessings or some external idea of success. We are talking about bearing spiritual fruit—fruit that comes forth from our lives as a result of the presence of the Holy Spirit, fruit that others can eat. Does the Sabbath Principle have any bearing on our spiritual fruitfulness?

The Scriptures portray a clear relationship between spiritual fruitfulness and the Sabbath Principle. In Isaiah 58, God promises to make Israel fruitful. This is obviously an Old Testament passage, but the New Testament makes it clear that the promises God gave Israel have direct application to His New Testament people today (see 1 Corinthians 10:11). The New Testament did not reinvent the spiritual wheel—it simply built new revelation on the strong foundation of Old Testament revelation. So it is perfectly valid for us to look to the prophet Isaiah for a connection between fruitfulness and the Sabbath Principle.

In Isaiah 58, the Lord declares to His people that they must not fast for purely religious reasons. Israel's fasting and service to the Lord was to have a much deeper meaning:

"Is not this the fast that I have chosen? To loose the bands of wickedness, to undo the heavy burdens, and to let the oppressed go free, and that ye break every yoke? Is it not to deal thy bread to the hungry, and that thou bring the poor that are cast out to thy house? When thou seest the naked, that thou cover him; and that thou hide not thyself from thine own flesh? Then shall thy light break forth as the morning, and thine health shall spring forth speedily: and thy righteousness shall go before thee; the glory of the LORD shall be thy reward. Then shalt thou call, and the LORD shall answer; thou shalt cry, and he shall say, 'Here I am.' If thou take away from the midst of thee the yoke, the putting forth of the finger, and speaking vanity; and if thou draw out thy soul to the hungry, and satisfy the afflicted soul; then shall thy

light rise in obscurity, and thy darkness be as the noon day: and the LORD shall guide thee continually, and satisfy thy soul in drought, and make fat thy bones: and thou shalt be like a watered garden, and like a spring of water, whose waters fail not. And they that shall be of thee shall build the old waste places: thou shalt raise up the foundations of many generations; and thou shalt be called, The repairer of the breach, The restorer of paths to dwell in. If thou turn away thy foot from the sabbath, from doing thy pleasure on my holy day; and call the sabbath a delight, the holy of the Lord, honourable; and shalt honour him, not doing thine own ways, nor finding thine own pleasure, nor speaking thine own words: then shalt thou delight thyself in the Lord; and I will cause thee to ride upon the high places of the earth, and feed thee with the heritage of Jacob thy father: for the mouth of the Lord hath spoken it." (Isaiah 58:6-14)

Usually when we read this chapter we stop at verse 12, but I would like to suggest that the Sabbath Principle found in verses 13 and 14 is an important part of Isaiah's entire message. The promise comes to the people that the Lord will guide them and help them in their time of need. He then promises that they will be like a well-watered garden and like springs of water that never fail. That is clearly a promise of fruitfulness.

The condition for the Lord's blessings resulting in great fruitfulness is the faithful keeping of the Sabbath. The application of the Sabbath Principle was to lead to fruitfulness. In the context of rebuking the people for their heartless religiosity He exhorts them to keep the Sabbath. Therefore, He must be referring to more than just a purely religious Sabbath-keeping. There is evidently a spiritual principle at stake in this powerful prophecy.

In fact, some would mistakenly claim that the Sabbath Principle is purely an aspect of the Mosaic Law and therefore not relevant to the new covenant. However, the Sabbath Principle began long before the Mosaic covenant.

The Sabbath Principle began in Genesis 2. Before God made a covenant with Moses on Mount Sinai, He defined the principle of the Sabbath. This principle was given by God and modeled by God at the end of the week of creation.

"Thus the heavens and the earth were finished, and all the host of them. And on the seventh day God ended his work which he had made; and he rested on the seventh day from all his work which he had made. And God blessed the seventh day, and sanctified it; because that in it he had rested from all his work which God created and made." (Genesis 2:1-3)

On the seventh and final day of creation God established a principle of rest. There are four things that took place on that seventh day:

1. God Ended His Work.

He labored for six days and then He ended His labor on the seventh.

2. God Rested.

You would not imagine that almighty God would need to rest, but that is what the Scriptures declare. On the seventh day God entered into His own rest.

3. God Sanctified the Seventh Day.

He set the seventh day apart for a holy purpose.

4. God Blessed the Seventh Day.

The seventh day was to be a day of blessing for those who would enter into the rest of that day.

Genesis 2 reveals that one out of seven days belongs to the Lord and that the seventh day has been sanctified and set apart by the Lord as a day of rest and blessings. It is therefore to be a day when God's people cease from their own labors and enter into the rest and blessings of the Lord.

ISRAEL AND THE SABBATH

This Sabbath Principle was then consistently taught and applied to the lives of God's people, from Adam to Noah, Abraham, and eventually the people of Israel. It did in fact become a part of God's covenant relationship with His people and we can learn some important principles by studying the role of the Sabbath in God's relationship with His people.

Here are some Scriptures concerning Israel and the Sabbath:

"And the Lord spake unto Moses, saying, speak thou also unto the children of Israel, saying, 'Verily my sabbaths ye shall keep: for it is a sign between me and you throughout your generations; that ye may know that I am the Lord that doth sanctify you. Ye shall keep the sabbath therefore; for it is holy unto you: every one that defileth it shall surely be put to death: for whosoever doeth any work therein, that soul shall be cut off from among his people. Six days may work be done; but in the seventh is the sabbath of rest, holy to the Lord: whosoever doeth any work in the sabbath day, he shall surely be put to death. Wherefore the children of Israel shall keep the sabbath, to observe the sabbath throughout their generations, for a perpetual covenant. It is a sign between me and the children of Israel forever: for in six days the Lord made heav-

en and earth, and on the seventh day he rested, and was refreshed.' And he gave unto Moses, when he had made an end of communing with him upon mount Sinai, two tables of testimony, tables of stone, written with the finger of God." (Exodus 31:12-18)

"And God spake all these words, saying, 'I am the Lord thy God, which have brought thee out of the land of Egypt, out of the house of bondage. Thou shalt have no other gods before me. . . .'Remember the sabbath day, to keep it holy. Six days shalt thou labour, and do all thy work: but the seventh day is the sabbath of the Lord thy God: in it thou shalt not do any work, thou, nor thy son, nor thy daughter, thy manservant, nor thy maidservant, nor thy cattle, nor thy stranger that is within thy gates: for in six days the Lord made heaven and earth, the sea, and all that in them is, and rested the seventh day: wherefore the Lord blessed the sabbath day, and hallowed it.'" (Exodus 20:1-3, 8-11)

"And on the sabbath day two lambs of the first year without spot, and two tenth deals of flour for a meat offering, mingled with oil, and the drink offering thereof: this is the burnt offering of every sabbath, beside the continual burnt offering, and his drink offering." (Numbers 28:9,10)

Dedicating the seventh day of the week to the Lord was the seal of the covenant relationship between God and His people, Israel. In fact, those who refused to keep the Sabbath were to be cut off from that relationship. The Ten Commandments, the very foundation of the Law, lists a clear commandment about keeping the Sabbath. Because God had entered into His own rest on the seventh day of creation, the people were to cease from their labors and enter into the Lord's rest on the seventh day as well.

The Sabbath day was also to include certain offerings. Two lambs were to be offered to the Lord, signifying the offering of the Lamb of God, the Lord Jesus Christ, as the way in which we must enter into God's rest. These lambs were to be offered as a burnt offering to the Lord as a sign of Israel's dedication to the Lord. The burnt offering was to be accompanied by a drink offering, giving a picture of the people feeding upon the word of God. These offerings were to be given to the Lord on every Sabbath day.

A DAY OF REST

The word "Sabbath" simply means, "rest, cessation from work, ending your own work." Keeping the Sabbath day means that we have ceased from our own works and are dedicating a period of time to the Lord, who is our Sabbath. Christ is our Sabbath and we can celebrate the Sabbath Principle only because of Him. As we come before Him we will find rest for our souls. This was clearly pictured in God's relationship with Israel. When they came before the Lord, ceased from their labors, and worshiped Him in the prescribed way, the Lord blessed them and gave them rest.

Have you ever noticed that you can be very weary from a difficult week of labor, come into the house of the Lord on the Lord's day, worship Him not out of tradition, but from your heart, and before long you find yourself being refreshed? In the presence of the Lord we find rest for our souls. The mountainous problems we had been facing before we came into the house of the Lord suddenly seem to shrink in the light of His presence. They take on their proper perspective in view of eternity and the Lord gives us the spiritual strength we need to enter into another six days of fruitful labor.

Let me repeat that from my own experience, I have never seen an exception—whenever anyone begins to take the Lord's day lightly, they are headed for a spiritual downward spiral. I am not talking about occasional legitimate reasons a person would have to miss assembling together on the Lord's day. We all take vacations or visit relatives from time to time. I am talking about people getting caught up in their own interests, prosperity, and goals, deliberately choosing to forsake the Lord's day in order to have one more day to do their own thing. This is an obvious sign that the Lord's priorities are no longer their priorities. They are not relying on the Lord to be their provider. They do not realize that with the Lord, they lack nothing. They have centered their lives around their own goals and doing their own thing in their own way. When that happens, they will not experience the Lord's rest. The blessings of the Lord will decrease in their lives and they will begin to experience spiritual barrenness. That individual or family has begun a serious downward spiral that will eventually result in spiritual death.

Please understand that I am not focusing in on a specific day as an end in itself. I want us to see the principle of the Sabbath day and I want us to see how that principle applies to us in the Twenty-first century. We are living in a day when understanding and respect for the Lord's day is almost unheard of. The Sabbath Principle is no longer a part of the Christian mindset. Gathering together on the Lord's day has become something we do on Sundays to be religious. That is exactly what happened in Israel. They continued to keep the law, but their heart was no longer in it. This eventually resulted in their hearts being attached to their idols rather than to the Lord. As a result, they spent forty years in the desert.

Ezekiel 20 shows that the reason Israel spent forty years in the wilderness, under the wrath of God, unfruitful, and having wasted a whole generation was because they would not keep the Sabbath day as a sign of the covenant relationship with their God. When I read that Scripture from Ezekiel, I am forced to conclude that the Lord was very interested in what His people did on the Sabbath. Starting on the seventh day of creation, He set a particular day in the week aside to bless His people and give them rest. But, if they did not respond and keep that one day holy, then they would not experience the blessings of the Lord and their lives would become unfruitful.

THE JEWISH SABBATH

In discussing the Sabbath Principle we should take a look at the Jewish Sabbath. How did Jewish people typically keep the Sabbath day?

1. **On the Sabbath Day, No Personal Work or Business Was to Be Done.**

2. **Nothing Was to Be Done Just for Personal Pleasure on the Sabbath.**

3. **It Was a Day When the True Jew Delighted in Jehovah and His Law.**

4. **They Were to Sacrifice Two Lambs Every Sabbath.**

They were to worship the Lord in the prescribed way. According to Hebrews 13:15, New Testament sacrifices involve the fruit of our lips–a sacrifice of praise to the Lord. 1 Peter 2:5 says that we come to offer spiritual sacrifices. The Lord is well pleased with such sacrifices. In that day, however, they sacrificed lambs as worship to the Lord.

5. **They Assembled Together on the Sabbath.**

6. **The Sabbath Was a Time of Celebration.**

In the Sabbath celebration they sang psalms and songs.

7. They Then Read and Taught from the Scriptures.

We have an example in Luke 4. Jesus went into the synagogue, as was His custom, picked up the Scriptures and read from Isaiah 61, claiming that God had anointed Him to preach the Gospel to the poor. The Scriptures had a prominent role in every Sabbath celebration.

8. They Prayed on the Sabbath.

Israelites offered many prayers of petition and thanksgiving to God on the Sabbath.

9. On the Sabbath Day They Also Reached Out to the Poor and the Needy.

10. They Rested their Physical Bodies After the Toils of the Week.

The Sabbath was ultimately a day of rest.

The elements of the Jewish Sabbath celebration sound very much like a New Testament Lord's day gathering—we come together to worship, sing, hear the word of God, and pray.

JESUS AND THE SABBATH

When we come to the New Testament period, we see the development of what the Israelite people call the "Talmud." The Talmud is a compilation of regulations that were to govern the people's actions. There are 1,521 rules governing the Sabbath in the Talmud. The early rabbis tried to restrict the people on the Sabbath as much as possible. They understood that the reason the people had gone into captivity was their refusal to keep the Sabbath. So the Pharisees and scribes developed 1,521 specific descriptions of what the people could and could not do on the Sabbath. It was these additional traditions added to the Sabbath that Jesus objected to. In an attempt to enforce covenant loyalty, legalism had come into Judaism. Jesus came to fulfill the law and so rejected the legalistic solution of the rabbis.

There is a very important difference between legalism and obedience: Obedience comes from the heart, legalism comes from the mind only, not from the heart. Legalism is enforced by fear. Obedience takes place because of love.

Matthew 12 provides an example of this legalism.

"At that time Jesus went on the sabbath day through the corn; and his disciples were an hungred, and began to pluck the ears of corn and to eat. But when the Pharisees saw it, they said unto him, 'Behold, thy disciples do that which is not lawful to do upon the sabbath day.' But he said unto them, 'Have ye not read what David did, when he was an hungred, and they that were with him; how he entered into the house of God, and did eat the shewbread, which was not lawful for him to eat, neither for them which were with him, but only for the priests? Or have ye not read in the law, how that on the sabbath days the priests in the temple profane the sabbath, and are blameless? But I say unto you, That in this place is one greater than the temple. But if ye had known what this meaneth, I will have mercy, and not sacrifice, ye would not have condemned the guiltless. For the Son of man is Lord even of the sabbath day.'" (Matthew 12:1-8)

The Son of Man is the Lord of the Sabbath. In other words, the Son of Man is the object and reason for the Sabbath. Keeping the Sabbath is not just a religious tradition; it is an act of worship to the Lord. It is a day set aside for God's people to come together and meet with the Lord of the Sabbath.

Jesus was constantly in trouble with the Pharisees and scribes concerning His conduct on the Sabbath. Never once was He violating the principle of the Sabbath, but by challenging all the traditions that had been added to the Sabbath, Jesus was always at odds with the religious leaders of His day. The people were under tremendous bondage to these Sabbath traditions, they could not care for their most basic needs. Jesus did not follow those traditions, but in going against them, He never violated the Sabbath Principle

THE NEW COVENANT SABBATH

In discussing the Sabbath, we must ultimately come around to our own application of the principle. How does all the teaching about the Sabbath apply to us? Why do we worship on Sunday, instead of Saturday, as they did in the Old Testament?

The Sabbath Principle was instituted by God, not man. God designed it to be a blessing for His people. It was to be a sign that His people were trusting in Him alone for rest. As a result, I have found that whenever this principle is consciously and unnecessarily violated (when a believer becomes so dedicated to his own agenda, pleasure, and goals that he no longer sets aside one day a week as a special day of worship and rest) spiritual problems are in store for him. His relationship with the Lord and his overall fruitfulness are drastically affected.

By the time we come to the New Testament period, the Jewish Talmud had added 1,521 very specific restrictions to keeping the Sabbath. The rabbis turned the principle of the Sabbath into a crude legalistic system that was a source of religious bondage for the people. As mentioned above, Jesus did not feel it necessary to honor these traditions, but He did honor the principle of the Sabbath. But this raises a few questions in our mind:

1. Why Not Keep the Jewish Sabbath?

Because it is impossible to keep the whole law. The law came to be a schoolmaster:

> *"Wherefore the law was our schoolmaster to bring us unto Christ, that we might be justified by faith."* (Galatians 3:24)

If we attempt to keep the Jewish Sabbath in a very literal way, we will have to sacrifice two lambs, avoid all work (even if it means great hardship to us and our family), attend a church close by since travel would be limited to two thousand yards, and avoid carrying anything heavy. That is just a small part of it. Not following all of it would result in excommunication. The Jewish Sabbath had its place in the Old Testament economy and in the Mosaic covenant. In Galatians 5:3 Paul says, *"For I testify again to every man that is circumcised, that he is a debtor to do the whole law."* If we try to return to keeping the old law, including the old Sabbath, we will be indebted to keeping the entire law. And if we break one part of the law, we will be guilty of breaking the whole law. The penalty of breaking the law of God is death. Jesus has come to give us life and to write His laws on our changed hearts. To attempt to return to the old law would remove us from the grace of God.

2. Why Did Jesus Keep the Sabbath?

He did not keep all the traditions of the elders, but He did keep the Jewish Sabbath. He worshiped on the Sabbath, taught on the Sabbath, healed on the Sabbath, and reached out to help people in need on the Sabbath. Jesus kept the old Jewish Sabbath every Saturday. Why? *"But when the fullness of the time was come, God sent forth his Son, made of a woman, made under the law, to redeem them that were under the law, that we might receive the adoption of sons"* (Galatians 4:4-5). When Jesus came, He was under the Law. Jesus was under the Mosaic covenant. He came to fulfill the Law and so had to live it out perfectly. This meant that He had to keep the Sabbath in the prescribed Old Testament way.

3. Why Did the Apostles Keep the Jewish Sabbath?

Paul said in Romans 1:16 that the Gospel was to be preached *"to the Jew first"* and the most logical place to do that was in the Jewish synagogue where the people gathered every Sabbath day. If the Gospel was to be preached to the Jew first, it had to be preached in the synagogue on the Jewish Sabbath. And that is exactly what the apostles did. They were involved in a transition period. The saints in the early church often met on the Jewish Sabbath because they were trying to reach out to the Jews.

4. When Did the Jewish Sabbath-Keeping End?

"And you, being dead in your sins and the uncircumcision of your flesh, hath he quickened together with him, having forgiven you all trespasses; blotting out the handwriting of ordinances that was against us, which was contrary to us, and took it out of the way, nailing it to his cross; and having spoiled principalities and powers, he made a shew of them openly, triumphing over them in it. Let no man therefore judge you in meat, or in drink, or in respect of an holyday, or of the new moon, or of the sabbath days: which are a shadow of things to come; but the body is of Christ." (Colossians 2:13-17)

The Cross brought the end of the Jewish Sabbath-keeping. When Jesus Christ came, all of the regulations that controlled the Mosaic economy, including the keeping of the Sabbath, ended. They were nailed to the cross. The old covenant came to an end and a new covenant was instituted.

5. Which Covenant Are We Under Now?

We are under the new covenant:

> *"And as they were eating, Jesus took bread, and blessed it, and brake it, and gave it to his disciples, and said, 'Take, eat; this is my body.' And he took the cup, and gave thanks, and gave it to them, saying, 'Drink ye all of it; for this is my blood of the new testament, which is shed for many for the remission of sins. But I say unto you, I will not drink henceforth of this fruit of the vine, until that day when I drink it new with you in my Father's kingdom.'"* (Matthew 26:26-29)

This was just before Jesus' death on the cross. He was saying that the bread and the wine of the Passover meal were symbolic of what He was about to do in instituting the new covenant. He then said that He would not partake of the new covenant meal with them again until He did it in His kingdom. The kingdom of God can only be entered into by the new birth. We gain entrance into God's kingdom under the new covenant by being born again by the Spirit of God. So it is clear that we are now under a new covenant.

In Acts 15 we see this very issue being discussed in what was probably one of the most crucial moments in the early church. This issue almost divided the early church. Luke says that there was a great dissension: *"When therefore Paul and Barnabas had no small dissension and disputation with them"* (Acts 15:2). It was not just a pleasant little chat.

What was the problem? On one side of the issue were those who wanted the new Gentile converts to first enter into the old Mosaic covenant. Paul withstood them, claiming that they were now under a new covenant. As a result, a major council of the apostles was called to discuss this situation.

The question was, "Is circumcision and Sabbath-keeping still in effect?" Some of them were saying, "Absolutely! That's what was given to Moses and it still applies to us today. Maybe we accept Jesus as the Messiah but we are still under the Mosaic covenant." But Paul said, "No way! That day is over and that covenant has been replaced by a new one."

After all, Jeremiah had prophesied about a new covenant. They all knew that there was something new coming from the Lord. They also knew that the Scriptures had prophesied the day when the Sabbath would cease, *"I will also cause all her mirth to cease, her feast days, her new moons, and her sabbaths, and all her solemn feasts"* (Hosea 2:11). The debate was heated and long, but finally they came to a conclusion that was good to the Holy Spirit and to all the brethren. James stood up to answer this problem by quoting the prophet Amos:

> *"And after they had held their peace James answered, saying, 'Men and brethren, hearken unto me: Simeon hath declared how God at the first did visit the Gentiles, to take out of them a people for his name. And to this agree the words of the prophets; as it is written, After this I will return, and will build again the tabernacle of David, which is fallen down; and I will build again the ruins thereof, and I will set it up: That the residue of men might seek after the Lord, and all the Gentiles, upon whom my name is called, saith the Lord, who doeth all these things. Known unto God all his works from the beginning of the world. Wherefore my sentence is, that we trouble not them, which from among the Gentiles are turned to God: But that we write unto them, that they abstain from pollutions of idols, and from fornication, and from things strangled, and from blood."* (Acts 15:13-20)

James quoted Amos 9:11 concerning the tabernacle of David. That tabernacle was a place where all the people could come before the presence of God without the usual restrictions. The Mosaic restriction of entrance to the Holy of Holies was suspended in the tabernacle of David. All the priests, not just the high priests, could come before the Ark of the Covenant. The Lord declared through Amos, "I am going to build it again," and establish the new covenant.

The Council of Jerusalem could have easily added the requirements of circumcision and Sabbath-keeping to the new Gentile converts. But they did not. Instead, *"it seemed good to the Holy Ghost, and to us, to lay upon you no greater burden than these necessary things"* (Acts 15:28).

The council revealed that they were no longer under the Mosaic covenant. God allowed a prophetic generation during the reign of David to demonstrate His desire that all men be able to come before His presence and seek Him without legalistic restrictions. We are still under the covering of the new covenant when all men are to know the Lord. We all have direct access into His presence. And as participants in the new covenant we are no longer obligated to keep the Jewish Sabbath.

6. All of the Ten Commandments Are Repeated in the New Testament Except the Fourth.

The fourth, the keeping of the Sabbath, is not mentioned anywhere in the New Testament. It was the seal of the Mosaic covenant and therefore did not have a specific role in the new covenant.

THE LORD'S DAY

Why do we even keep Sunday as the Lord's day? For the Jews, the Sabbath was Saturday. In the early church, the Lord's Day became Sunday. Why the change? Let me give you some biblical and historical reasons:

1. Because Christ's Resurrection Took Place on the First Day of the Week.

The most important event in human history was Christ's resurrection. His death was important, but if He had not been raised from the dead, our salvation would not be possible. That makes the day He rose again a very important day. Symbolically, this principle was foreshadowed in Leviticus 23:11 with the waving of the firstfruits on the first day of the week. Jesus Christ is the firstfruits offering from the dead. He is our firstfruits who came to bring many sons to glory. This all took place on the first day of the week.

2. The Holy Spirit, the Seal of the New Covenant, Was Poured Out on the First Day of the Week, on the Day of Pentecost.

Pentecost means "fifty." In Leviticus 23:15-16, the day after the seventh Sabbath, the fiftieth day, was to be the day of Pentecost. Symbolically, not only was the resurrection predicted on the first day of the week, but so was the outpouring of the Holy Spirit.

3. The Early Disciples Met and Broke Bread on the First Day of the Week After the Resurrection of Christ (Acts 20:7).

4. The Early Believers Gathered Together and Gave Offerings on the First Day of the Week (1 Corinthians 16:1-2).

Already in the first generation of the church the saints had a regular practice of gathering on the first day.

5. Some Claim That It Was the Roman Emperor Constantine and the Imperial Catholic Church That Changed the Day of Worship from Saturday to Sunday.

However, the historical evidence shows that the early church worshiped on Sunday from the earliest days. Let's look at some of the writings of the early church fathers concerning their worship on Sunday. The epistles of Ignatius were written in AD 107. Ignatius was a pupil of the apostles and was commended by Polycarp who was a friend of the Apostle John. He wrote, "And after the observance of the Sabbath, let every friend of Christ keep the Lord's day as a festival, the resurrection day, the queen and chief of all days." It was true that some of the early Christians participated in the Jewish Sabbath since the Gospel was to be preached to the Jews first. Then they gathered together on the first day of the week for the Christian celebration. In the earliest writings, Sunday was referred to as "the Lord's day," the day He rose from the dead. Ignatius goes on to say, "those who were concerned with old things have come to newness of confidence, no longer keeping the Sabbath, but living according to the Lord's day, as which our life as risen again through him depends."

Justin Martyr, who wrote in A.D. 145, said that, "Sunday is the day on which we all hold our common assembly. Because it is the first day of the week and Jesus Christ our savior on that same day rose from the dead."

In the second century, the Apostolic Constitution instructed the people that "on the day of the resurrection of the Lord, that is the Lord's day, assemble yourselves together without fail, giving thanks to God and praising him for those mercies God has bestowed upon us through Christ."

Tertullian wrote in A.D. 200, "he who argues for the Sabbath-keeping and circumcision must hold that Adam and Abel and the just of old times observed these things. We observe the day of the Lord's resurrection, laying aside our worldly business." History shows us that the early church worshiped God on Sunday.

I believe that the enemy has been working to destroy the application of the Sabbath Principle in the church today. He wants to get us bogged down in a debate over specific days and lose sight of the principle. We do not worship the day, we worship the Lord of the day. The whole purpose of the day is to set aside time to worship the Lord.

The Bible warns us that we are not to be pressed into the world's mold and to adopt the world's ways. Instead we are to be transformed by the renewing of our minds.

It is not that many years ago in America that very few businesses were open on Sunday. Today malls are bustling. I was raised in a time when the Lord's day was special. As a child I could not do as I did on the other days of the week—and I loved Sundays. We did a lot of wonderful things with the family. We gathered for great feasts and times of fellowship. There was always something different and special about the Lord's day.

HONORING THE LORD'S DAY

The Sabbath Principle is in the Bible from cover to cover. We need to be so in love with the Lord and His ways that it is our joy and delight to set aside one entire day a week to cease from the pursuit of our own pleasures, work, and goals to focus solely on worshiping the Lord. If our daily delight is in the Lord, His Word, His ways, and the family of God, then we will not object to setting aside the first day of the week as a special day to the Lord.

I believe we ought to teach our children to honor the Lord's day and to teach it first of all by example. I remember that whenever the house of the Lord was open on the Lord's day, nothing could keep our family from being there. It did not matter if there was an ice storm or blizzard or anything else, my mother, father, two brothers, and I got into the car and drove through the weather in Minnesota to head for the house of God. Even if no other families were there, Mom, Dad, and three little Iverson brothers were there to worship and serve the Lord. It was a time we had set aside to honor the Lord. I grew up delighting in Sundays. I did not understand all the ramifications as a child. I just knew it was a special day. I had to treat the day with respect. I thank God for parents that taught me that there is meaning and fruitfulness in life when we serve the Lord and give Him that one day a week.

The Lord will guide us if we can just focus our attention on Him. The world has so many distractions. We walk through a real mud pit all week long. It is wonderful to walk into the house of the Lord where there is love and wholesomeness and sit for a few hours and worship the Lord, open His Word and enjoy the fellowship of the brethren. That, to me, is the most blessed time of the week.

There is a principle involved in the Sabbath. Keeping one day a week holy unto the Lord brings the blessings of the Lord. It is not legalistic. He is not going to kill us if we do not do it. But the Lord is calling us back to Himself—to the kind of covenant relationship signified by the Sabbath Principle. The Lord is calling His church once again: "Come, let's spend this day together. Come and let me feed you the Word and strengthen you. Let me love you and support you."

It is no wonder we are to love this day. This is the day we have set aside of all the days in the week to be special, to be holy unto the Lord. When this revering truth is respected in our lives and in our congregations, God's heart is blessed. He gladly responds by blessing us personally.

CHAPTER EIGHT

Guiding Truth:
Spiritual Authority

We have all heard the phrase, "blessings in disguise." There are many things in life that, at first glance, seem undesirable but turn out to be extremely beneficial—in short, a blessing. If we told a teenager that the greatest thing that could happen to him at that important time of his life is to have good discipline and loving authority, he would think we were crazy. But it would be the truth. Loving authority is a great blessing in disguise.

Authority is God-given, and provides the foundation and structure of a happy life. It is good for children to submit to the parental authority of their father and mother. It is also good for citizens to respect the civil authorities of their land, since the Bible makes it clear that God established civil authority. World rulers, good and bad, cannot rise or fall without the aid of God (see Daniel 4:17; Romans 13:1; Proverbs 21:1; John 19:11; Psalm 75:6-7; 1 Samuel 2:7,10; Luke 1:52, 1 Kings 14:14). Authority is a God-ordained institution that is meant to be a blessing in every aspect of our lives.

A BIBLICAL PRECEDENT

This principle of divinely instituted authority was established early under the Mosaic covenant. It was to be taken so seriously that those who did not obey were to be put to death.

> *"According to the sentence of the law which they shall teach thee, and according to the judgment which they shall tell thee, thou shalt do . . . And the man that will do presumptuously, and will not hearken unto the priest that standeth to minister there before the Lord thy god, or unto the judge, even that man shall die."* (Deuteronomy 17:11-12)

The new covenant local church has also been given authority by God. Those who exercise that authority are called rulers (Greek: *hegoumenos, proistamenos*), elders, (Greek: *presbyterous*), and overseers or bishops (Greek: *episkopoi*). The apostle Paul enumerates five distinct offices these authority figures can hold: apostles, prophets, evangelists, pastors, and teachers (see Ephesians 4:11). The exercise of authority by these men is vital to church life, church growth, and church planting.

THE MEANING OF AUTHORITY

The word "authority" is translated in the King James from three Greek words: *exousia, epitage, hyperoche*. They deal with the privilege and right to do something, the injunctive and communicative aspect of ruling (see Matthew 21:24; Acts 26:12; 2 Corinthians 10:8; Titus 2:15).

For our study, a companion word to consider is the word "power." It is translated from the Greek words *dunamis*, and *ischus*. Some commentators contrast "authority" (the right to do something), with "power" (the strength or ability to do something). There may be some merit to this difference in meaning. The King James, however, translates *exousia* as either authority or power. Power and authority are closely related. One minister compared power to the fire within the stove, and authority to the stove itself that controls and harnesses the fire for good use. The power of the Holy Spirit is given to all within the church and authorities are raised up by God to direct that power.

Think of authority as the banks of a river. Without borders to channel and control it, a river will be nothing more than a wide lake—having little affect on its world. But with banks that serve as guardians and directors for the water, a river becomes a powerful force. Water is water. How it affects the world depends on its ability to flow within banks. People are people. How we affect others depends on our ability to submit to proper authority.

MISUSE AND ABUSE OF AUTHORITY

It behooves us to give close attention to the topic of authority because of the importance it holds to our daily Christian lives. On the one hand, authority has been made too powerful. We have seen authority figures cruelly lead their followers to premature deaths. We have seen cult figures seduce their disciples into forsaking traditional values of purity. Some, in a state of paranoia, amass stockpiles of weaponry. There have been some who have notoriously claimed for themselves the title of "Messiah," manifest on earth again. Some cult leaders have even engaged in terrorism.

The evening news has told us of some who hold such a tight control over the minds of their disciples that they, on command, subject their own children to physical abuse and cruelty. A few leaders have even promoted child sexual abuse and sodomy.

We cannot point the finger of accusation solely at eastern religions, Christian cults, or deviant communal sects. There has been authoritarian corruption in mainline Christian organizations, as well. "Down home" churches have been shocked by the scandalous abuse of authority figures.

On the other hand, we know of those who refuse to follow any and all authority. There are extreme groups acting outside and against the church. We have been confronted with movements led by individuals who display a "just Jesus and me" attitude. They explain that every man should live for himself, "Because authority has been abused!"

Satan is doing all he can to take away that which is good, beneficial, and important by attacking the spiritual authority over Christ's churches. He discredits the idea of authority by inspiring abuses and tempting those in authority positions. He undercuts authority by spreading the spirit of rebellion. He subtly chips away at it by propagating the mentality of self-reliance and self-sufficiency. The reason he fights it so much is because of the great potential for good it can have in expanding and establishing the kingdom of God. Spiritual authority is an immense blessing to those who joyfully submit to it.

CHALLENGES TO AUTHORITY

Authority is challenged in our day very often. Our society views authority figures with a sense of distrust. From our parents to the president, authority is called into question as a general rule. Moses was one of the greatest leaders of the Jewish people, yet Acts 7:35 shows that his authority was constantly called into question. According to 1 Corinthians 9, the apostle Paul was questioned. Luke 20:2-4 states that Jesus Himself had his authority questioned. Both in our day and in the Bible, we will find that the authority figures we have endure the questioning of those they rule over.

When we realize that spiritual authority is a blessing from God to the church, then we will see stability in ministry, and meaningful structure for the body of believers. Growth and productivity will inevitably result.

GUIDELINES FOR SPIRITUAL AUTHORITY

Spiritual authority is to be in operation in the local church and the kingdom of God. However, to exercise authority properly and to keep abuse from occurring, there are a few principles we should keep in mind.

1. Be Merciful in Discipline.

Correction and discipline are a necessary part of growth, whether it be of children in a family, employees in a business, or believers in a church (see Hebrews 12:5-11; Proverbs 3:11-12; Revelation 3:19; 2 Timothy 3:16). Discipline, handled correctly, matures a person. People without discipline bring shame (see Proverbs 29:15); their evil spreads like gangrene (see 2 Timothy 2:17).

Jesus Christ spelled out the correct procedure for discipline in the church. Notice that there are different degrees of intensity in correction (see Matthew 18:15-20). In exercising spiritual authority in the area of discipline, we must not be too severe. In dealing with spiritual sins and spiritual backsliding, we must also be careful not to cause spiritual death.

The motive and intent of every act of correction is supposed to be "restoration." When there is repentance, we need to be merciful and gracious. Love covers things, it does not expose maliciously (see Proverbs 10:12; 1 Peter 4:8; Romans 4:7; Psalm 32:1).

"He that covereth a transgression seeketh love; but he that repeateth a matter separateth very friends." (Proverbs 17:9)

"Brethren, if a man be overtaken in a fault, ye which are spiritual, restore such an one in the spirit of meekness; considering thyself, lest thou also be tempted." (Galatians 6:1)

Sin must be dealt with—it cannot go unchecked. We cannot look the other way. That is not what is meant when it says to "cover" a transgression. We are to nip it in the bud whenever possible, but we are to do it with humility and meekness.

2. Be Meticulous in Word.

A leader's words are important. The words of a person in a position of respectability have a lot more authority than the rank and file. We must be very careful about this. When the president or a member of the cabinet holds a press conference or gives an address at a meeting, he usually reads a prepared statement. This is because thousands and millions of people will be jumping at every word and drawing conclusions from each phrase that is spoken. The president's speechwriters spend hours preparing and analyzing each sentence. Spontaneous remarks and off-the-cuff quips have ruined many careers of aspiring politicians. Some "cute" remarks have also endangered peaceful "foreign relations."

We must guard our words if we are in spiritual authority. It is a natural tendency for individuals to take what we have said and put more weight to them than we intended:

"Death and life are in the power of the tongue." (Proverbs 18:21)

"Whoso keepeth his mouth and his tongue keepeth his soul from troubles." (Proverbs 21:23)

Sometimes a person will approach me and say, "Pastor, do you remember when you talked to me in the hallway?" Immediately, I begin to get nervous. What did I say? Was I joking? Did they take it out of context? Some will tend to put their life on that word that comes out of our mouths, even when we are speaking during a "relaxed" conversation. I am really relieved when he finishes relating to me the incident by saying, "...and it really worked."

Not only is what we say in relaxed conversations important, but so is the spiritual advice, counseling, and prophetic words we give. I strongly urge that all prophecies be judged, and that out of "the mouth of two or three witnesses" everything be established (see 2 Corinthians 13:1; Matthew 18:16; Deuteronomy 19:15; 1 Corinthians 14:29). Our words must be guarded.

3. Be Friendly in Relationships.

Relationship, not hierarchy, is the basis of spiritual authority. Holding a position, filling an office, or being elected to a place of importance is not how spiritual elders are made—they must earn it! One qualifies to be a leader by developing relationships. A spiritual leader has a working relationship with those over whom he has authority.

Some try to maintain their position over their congregation by a spirit of oppression. There is a fine line here. They may not violate anything in the Bible, yet there is an oppressive spirit. The way they introduce new needs, the manner in which they discipline, the inflection in their announcements, all give off an offensiveness—a sort of detachment or an at-arms-length mood. That type of leader is hard for people to follow.

A good husband does not rule over his wife and children without their input. They would soon lose respect for him if he did—a lack of cooperation would set in. A tactful, sensitive spirit goes a lot farther than laying down a set of guidelines in an oppressive manner and walking out.

I have found that people do not mind working and rallying around the vision of God. They will sacrifice, but not under a spirit of oppression! It dampens their enthusiasm quickly. Leaders will lose their relationship with the people if they operate with a spirit of oppression—and once a relationship is diminished, everything else starts falling apart.

Solomon wrote, *"faithful are the wounds of a friend"* (Proverbs 27:6). Correction and rebuke are more palatable when they come from a "friend," from someone with whom we have a friendly relationship. They are rarely accepted beneficially from an authority figure with an oppressive spirit, even when he is one hundred percent correct in his rebuke. But if that authority figure is also friendly, the correction will hit its mark and have a positive result.

4. Be Mutual in Recognition.

Real spiritual authority is recognized, not imposed. It can never be forced onto believers. Sheep are not driven like cattle; they are led, and the sheep willingly follow. Believers have the free will to decide to follow or not. Nothing can violate the freedom of choice that every person has in the church. Each person must be fully persuaded in his own conscience about matters of Christian commitment. The sheep must recognize and accept those in authority. Those in authority must also recognize and give themselves to the sheep. There is a two-way commitment between them that is willingly given.

After Joshua had established a foothold as the leader of Israel, the people were approached and confronted with a choice of commitment: *"Choose you this day whom ye will serve"* (Joshua 24:15). People in a local church must also make the choice of commitment. They must want to be there, and flow together in unity under the spiritual authority. If for some reason a particular family cannot, in good conscience, flow with the leadership, they have the right to leave and be planted in another local church. It is sad sometimes to see a family go, but sometimes it is necessary. The leadership cannot force its authority upon them and make them stay.

There are other times when some will not accept the God-given authority over them, and refuse their counsel and teaching. Some will not accept the decisions of the oversight that they should. By so doing, they are often removing themselves from under the umbrella of spiritual protection, and opening themselves to needless consequences. Still, they must be allowed that freedom. When a family does not recognize and respect the authority over them, they lose out on the many benefits that could come through submission. They often run away from the very help that God has sent them!

What can we do to prevent this from happening? Teach the people their responsibility towards authority. Here is a partial list:

- Pray and intercede for all that are in authority
  (see 1 Timothy 2:1-2).
- Be thankful for God-given authority (see 1 Timothy 2:1-2).
- Bestow honor on new elders (see Numbers 27:20).
- Pay attention to leadership (see 1 Thessalonians 5:12).
- Esteem them very highly in love (see 1 Thessalonians 5:13).
- Be subject unto them, as men appointed by God
  (see Romans 13:1).
- Remember them that rule (see Hebrews 13:7).
- Obey them that have the rule, and submit (see Hebrews 13:17).
- Salute all of them (see Hebrews 13:24).
- Give double honor to those that rule well (see 1 Timothy 5:17).
- Do not accept gossip without proof (see 1 Timothy 5:19).
- Rebuke those who sin (see 1 Timothy 5:20).

Responsiveness and appreciation by the sheep bring out the best in a shepherd. The effectiveness of spiritual elders depends on the people "backing them up." When the people flow together in unity, the leadership is encouraged and relaxed. This happy state, in turn, releases them to concentrate more efficiently on the work of the ministry. Mutual respect leads to mutual blessing! What a joy it is to work with appreciative people. What a joy it also is to serve them.

5. Be Managerial in Operation.

Some parents tend to be domineering over their families. Their actions are threatening, manipulating, and dictatorial. They give commands instead of counsel, order instead of train, or scold instead of correct. These overbearing parents often produce children with undesirable character traits that are not socially productive.

They do not realize that the main goal in raising children is to instill in them the ability to make wise decisions and eventually be productive in society, and this is best accomplished by the parents being in the role of manager, not dictator. Parents are not simply to keep everything in control, under their thumbs, until the children are eighteen and then push them out into the world. Instead, they are couples who have been entrusted with a precious commodity that they are to wisely develop into mature adults, like themselves. They are held accountable to do this because they, like a manager, are under a higher authority themselves:

"All things are your's . . . And ye are Christ's; and Christ is God's." (1 Corinthians 3:21-23)

"The head of every man is Christ; and the head of the woman is the man; and the head of Christ is God." (1 Corinthians 11:3)

Parents are stewards of God's treasure and are to be faithful (see 1 Corinthians 4:2). They are to manage well, not as owners of the treasure, but only as temporary trustees. If they were the owners, they would have a right to be dictatorial; they would be the boss and have power to do anything they wish. Bosses are not accountable to anyone–they own the company. Managers are only middlemen who hold the important task of presenting the final product to the owner.

Just as successful parenting is based on parent behavior (not child behavior) so also is successful exercise of spiritual authority based upon the leadership's behavior. If the leadership is dictatorial and domineering, certain traits are going to surface in the congregation. The "iron hand" of the leader will stifle a true heart of loyalty. Loyalty will be given out of fear instead of desire. The authoritarian leader will limit opportunities for others to share in body ministry. He will frustrate those who have valuable counsel and want to serve. He will treat all other opinions or ideas as threats to his own position of authority. The domineering leader will be suspicious and pessimistic about the sheep, an attitude that trickles down among the sheep themselves. Suspicion and backbiting hinder the character development and maturation that should be occurring. The intimidation of this kind of ruler will suppress the fruit of the Spirit: peace, joy, love, etc. The whole environment of the church is affected.

As managers, leaders should remember that they are responsible to both God and those they lead for their actions. They are the middlemen God places to lead the people. As such, they are to treat the people with respect and dignity while developing them to become strong spiritual people in their own right.

6. Be Reliant on God for Provision.

I feel I should briefly mention another word of caution in the exercise of spiritual authority because the Bible mentions it repeatedly and because we see some abuse in this realm in present day churches—possessions and finances.

In 1 Corinthians 9:6-14, Paul reminds the Corinthians that God does not muzzle the ox while it is working. Likewise, those in authority should receive wages for their work. In addition, 1 Timothy 5:17 says that those who rule well are worthy of double honor.

Honor is often used in the Scriptures to mean financial support or remuneration. We are to "honor" the Lord with our first fruits, we are to "honor" our elderly parents by supporting them in old age (see Proverbs 3:9; Ephesians 6:2, compare with 1 Timothy 5:8), and here we are told to doubly honor those in spiritual authority. This is proper and just.

Some congregations still live by the old saying, though: "The Lord keep him (pastor) humble, and we will keep him poor!" Some may say that in jest, but it is a realistic fact in a lot of churches. Other churches have a tradition of hiring a pastor for a year or so, and then by a no-vote of confidence, place the minister and his family out on the street.

Because of this improper treatment by congregations, those in authority are overwhelmed by insecurity. Just like anyone who loses a job, it is a traumatic experience for those in authority to lose support and not be able to care for himself and his struggling family. It is this insecurity I would like to zero in on, because it has opened the door of temptation for many pastors or spiritual leaders.

Those in authority must prepare their minds to accept the fact that it is possible their service might not be fully appreciated. This should not discourage them to the point of quitting the ministry, nor yielding to the temptation to purloin riches.

The apostle Paul did not hesitate to receive financial support from the churches in Macedonia (see 2 Corinthians 11:9). However, in some churches, especially the church at Corinth in Achaia where financial matters created problems, Paul would not accept any support. Here he, along with Aquila and Priscilla, worked as a tent maker to support himself while he preached for a year and a half (see Acts 18:1-11). We are not quite sure what the money problems were, but we are told what Paul's attitude was:

"Giving no offence in any thing, that the ministry be not blamed; but in all things approving ourselves as the ministers of God, in

*much patience, in afflictions, in necessities . . . as poor, yet mak-
ing many rich; as having nothing, and yet possessing all things."*
(2 Corinthians 6:3-4,10)

*"Behold, the third time I am ready to come to you; and I will not
be burdensome to you: for I seek not your's, but you: for the children ought not to lay up for the parents, but the parents for the
children. And I will very gladly spend and be spent for you."*
(2 Corinthians 12:14,15)

Paul had the spiritual authority to receive wages and financial support from these people he ministered to, but his compassion was that
nothing be allowed to hinder the Gospel. He was willing to become a
pauper, that they might become rich. He should have been supported,
but he did not use or abuse his authority to demand it. He did not
abuse his spiritual authority.

Many young ministers get a taste of suffering and quit. They
change their mind about being called into the ministry. In this matter,
though, we must keep our trust in God, and not in uncertain riches
(see 1 Timothy 6:17).

On the other hand, some in spiritual authority have leaned in
another direction. They have made merchandise of the Gospel, driven
by this spirit of insecurity. That insecurity has given way to the spirit of
covetousness *"And through covetousness shall they with feigned words
make merchandise of you"* (2 Peter 2:3). Both responses show that the
one in spiritual authority does not rely on God for his provision. The
answer is to preach the Gospel with all authority and teach the flock to
properly support those who rule. If they do not live up to this responsibility, still remain faithful as a servant of Jesus Christ and rely upon
Him for provision.

7. Be Modest in Personal Appraisal.

Supernatural spiritual authority is powerful. Used correctly, it brings life. One would think that it would always be used for good. Who would deliberately want to produce death? However, a wise person once coined the phrase, "Power corrupts, and absolute power corrupts absolutely." For those in spiritual authority, it is good to have wise counsel that will remind them not to let their position go to their head. Or as Paul puts it, *"Take heed unto thyself, and unto the doctrine; continue in them: for in doing this thou shalt both save thyself, and them that hear thee"* (1 Timothy 4:16).

Without keeping an honest and realistic appraisal of himself, the spiritual leader will find it easy to fall into the error of Diotrephes, *"who loveth to have the preeminence"* (3 John 9). He must not think of himself *"more highly than he ought to think"* (Romans 12:3; see also Galatians 6:3). Instead, he should be cautious about how he receives compliments and praise for his work.

Besides wise counselors, there is something else that is essential to keeping those in spiritual authority "in line," and that is the fear of God. A spiritual leader must be walking in the presence of God so that he experiences the fear of God, *"He that ruleth over men must be just, ruling in the fear of God"* (2 Samuel 23:3).

Spiritual authority is God-given. We cannot think that we have absolute authority—that belongs to God; He is absolute power. That should strike a healthy fear in the heart of any leader. The heart that fears the Lord is the heart that is committed to the Lord, and in such a heart there is no room for compromise with evil (see Proverbs 8:13). Even the earthly walk of Christ was in fear of the Lord (see Isaiah 11:1-4), and that was the basis for His righteous "judging." He moved under the canopy of this fear of God (see Hebrews 5:7). How much more do we need the fear of God so we will not fall under the influence of the tempter (see Acts 9:31)? Without the fear of the Lord, we will capitulate. For people to respect our authority, we must show that we respect God's.

The fear of the Lord delivers us from all other fears: the fear of failure, the fear of man, and the fear of nature. No single aspect of the Christian life carries greater blessing with it than the fear of God. We especially need it to maintain a balance in the exercise of authority, to keep a correct perspective, and to remain humble and meek. With it and the reminder from others that all authority is God's, we will be able to keep a modest personal appraisal.

8. Be Miraculous in Conduct.

A God that is not all powerful is no God at all—it was only natural that when God came to earth in the man Jesus Christ, He confirmed His deity with supernatural acts. Jesus went into the desert to be tempted, and He *"returned in the power of the Spirit"* (Luke 4:14). Not only did He heal the sick, cast out demons, and feed multitudes miraculously, but the people were astonished at His doctrine, for *"His word was with power"* (Luke 4:32).

He then gave the twelve apostles *"power and authority over all devils, and to cure diseases. And he sent them to preach"* (Luke 9:1-2). On the day of Pentecost, this power was distributed to all believers (see Acts 1:8).

The Book of Acts records time and again how the preached Word was confirmed with signs following:

"And by the hands of the apostles were many signs and wonders wrought among the people." (Acts 5:12)

"And Stephen, full of faith and power, did great wonders and miracles among the people." (Acts 6:8)

"And the people with one accord gave heed unto those things which Philip spake, hearing and seeing the miracles which he did." (Acts 8:6)

"And God wrought special miracles by the hands of Paul." (Acts 19:11)

Paul taught several times that the preaching of the word was not to be flowery speech that appealed to man's wishes, but it was to come to the people in *"power, and in the Holy Ghost, and in much assurance"* (1 Thessalonians 1:5; see also 1 Corinthians 2:4; 4:19-20). On one occasion he listed signs, wonders, and mighty deeds as proof of his apostleship (see 2 Corinthians 12:12).

The great lack of respect for spiritual authority in society today is because of the absence of power that comes through the anointing of the Holy Spirit. Much of the rebellion toward the church is based on the feeling that it is authoritarian but has no real spiritual power, *"Having a form of godliness, but denying the power thereof"* (2 Timothy 3:5). Spiritual authority without spiritual power is like an army without weapons. *"The weapons of our warfare are not carnal, but mighty through God"* (2 Corinthians 10:4).

God has given leaders a great and glorious calling: to bring life where darkness reigns. The spiritual authority which God has bestowed on us is powerful. We must not cause disrespect for it by exercising it in word only. If we are going to exercise spiritual authority, we need to walk in the Spirit, be led by the Spirit, and be filled with the Spirit. God's church is a dynamic church, a church filled with the dynamic of the Spirit (see Acts 1:8).

People will have no problem respecting spiritual authorities when they are men moving in the Spirit and fear of God. The modern church can regain its respectability!

WE CAN DO IT!

Following these guidelines as we exercise our authority in the local churches will help in curbing abuses. It will provide a check-and-balance to an important aspect of church life. Spiritual authorities on earth reflect upon the real Authority in heaven, so it is important that we operate discreetly and with propriety. When we do, Christ will be glorified and exalted in the eyes of the people. This is our hearts' desire—that the Head of the church be glorified!

CHAPTER NINE

Inspiring Truth:
The Spirit of Prophecy

The spirit of prophecy makes us a prophetic people—a people that hear the voice of God and know His mind as it is expressed in an audible way. It is so crucial that we have an ear to hear what the Lord says to His people today, and in every generation. By having an ear to hear the voice of the Lord, we know where we have been, where we are now, and where we are going. Prophecy reveals our character, condition, mission, and destiny, and illuminates God's will in our lives.

VARIETY OF METHODS

A survey of the Bible reveals the fact that there are a variety of ways for God to convey the prophetic word. There are several methods of hearing from the Lord. He speaks to us in ways best suited for our hearing. Following is a summary of them:

1. The Lord Speaks to Us Through a "Spoken Prophetic Word."

In 1 Thessalonians 5:20, the Lord warns us to *"Despise not prophesyings."* Our spiritual sensitivity to the prophetic voice of the Holy Spirit is crucial in these days. We must not take lightly our need to hear from the Lord in this way.

As I look back on fifty years of ministry, I can see many times when a prophetic word has dramatically changed my life or kept me from harm. When the Holy Spirit spoke to me and gave me direction, it had an impact on my life that brought me into a whole new level of commitment to God. The course of my life was changed when the word of the Lord came.

We want the Holy Spirit to order our footsteps. Our heavenly Father wants to share His secrets with us—He wants to tell us the right way to walk. The Father delights in communicating with us. We too must delight in fellowship and communication with the Lord.

I have had about a dozen encounters with the word of the Lord that have changed my life. About every few years or so the Holy Spirit has spoken to me in a specific way concerning my life, and each time I was affected.

The Lord does not speak to me the same way each time. There have been times when a prophet pointed his finger at me and said, "Thus saith the Lord." At times it came as hands were laid upon me and the word of the Lord came. God does not have a certain way He speaks and works in every situation. The Lord meets us in many different ways to accomplish His will in our lives. The method is not the important thing, as long as God speaks.

2. The Lord Speaks Through the Scriptures.

When I refer to the word of the Lord, I am not talking about a word of revelation above and beyond the Bible. Any prophetic word must be under the authority of the written Word of God. If someone comes and says, "Thus saith the Lord," and the word he gives is not in harmony with the written Scriptures, simply reject it.

On the other hand, we cannot always open the Bible and find out specifically where to go and what to do in every situation of life. Specific needs for guidance and direction often require specific words from the Lord. There are not always Scriptures to tell us whether or not we should build a building or move from one place to another. We may find principles that relate to the issue we are struggling with, but contain no specific word of direction.

There have been times when the Lord has sovereignly brought a Scripture to me that leaped off the page, grabbed my spirit, and sounded in my soul like a trumpet from heaven. It was just as much a "Thus saith the Lord" as if a prophet had been speaking directly to me. The Lord focused a specific Scripture on my situation at a specific moment and it transformed my life.

When we were seeking the Lord about buying an old theater to move our church, the Lord led me to the book of Nehemiah in the middle of the night. He spoke to me in a living way out of chapter 7. One of the statements the Lord gave me was, *"Now the city was large and great: but the people are few therein"* (v. 4). The Lord gave me this word ahead of time. For five years we rattled around in our auditorium with just a handful of people. Every time I walked into that nearly empty building I would tend to get discouraged. Year after year, nothing seemed to cause the church to grow. But each time the Lord brought Nehemiah 7:4 back to mind and that word held me.

I am not advocating that every time we need direction from the Lord we just go to a single Scripture and make it our automatic guide. Our direction must come as a result of two or three witnesses (Deuteronomy 19:15). I am referring to times when the Holy Spirit sovereignly visits us and speaks clearly to us out of the Scriptures, at His initiative, not ours.

In addition, we cannot expect some kind of prophetic word every time we face a decision in life. But as we seek after God and open our heart to Him, He will be faithful to guide us. The Lord wants to give us direction, and one of the ways He will guide us is through the Scriptures.

3. The Lord Speaks to Our Inner Man.

When the Holy Spirit has been dealing with us and preparing our hearts, He may come to us and give an inner witness of His word, *"This is the way, walk ye in it"* (Isaiah 30:21). When the Lord speaks clearly to us in this way, it is just as powerful a prophetic word as it would be if a prophet spoke to us or the Lord revealed His will through the Scriptures. It is an anointed word, a voice out of heaven, directed to us.

4. The Lord Speaks Through Godly Counsel.

Godly counsel is the multitude of counselors. It is in this context that the Lord may give us a word of knowledge or a word of wisdom. Think of sitting across from a godly man or woman and suddenly being profoundly aware of the fact that out of his or her mouth comes a word from the Lord. It comes clearly and simply. We may even say, "Why didn't I think of that?" That word of counsel was just as much an anointed, prophetic word as it would have been any other way. We cannot lock God in some kind of box, His word can come to us in any number of ways.

5. The Lord Speaks by a Word of Instruction from Someone Who Is in Authority.

God will often use those who have authority over us to give us prophetic guidance and direction. It may come as the advice of parents to their children. God often uses our parents to give us spiritual direction and insight for our lives. Parents are a God-given institution with God-given authority.

The Lord may also give prophetic direction through local church overseers. The Lord gives certain people as gifts to the body of Christ and uses them to give direction to those people. While counsel given by those in spiritual authority is often not meant to be directional, God can use that counsel to direct us nonetheless. Someone in spiritual authority may have the word of the Lord for us.

Prophetic words come through a variety of methods, yet in every way it is the word of the Lord to us. The gift of prophecy to the church is not just for a few special zealots, God wants us to be prophetic people. Whether or not we are in authority or hold an office in the church, He desires for us to be prophetic in every aspect of our lives. We are to be prophetic conduits for God.

PROPHETIC PEOPLE

Prophetic people are described in Romans 13:

> *"And that, knowing the time, that now it is high time to awake out of sleep: for now is our salvation nearer than when we believed. The night is far spent, the day is at hand: let us therefore cast off the works of darkness, and let us put on the armor of light. Let us walk honestly, as in the day; not in rioting and drunkenness, not in clambering and wantonness, not in strife and envying: but put ye on the Lord Jesus Christ, and make not provision for the flesh to fulfill the lusts thereof."* (Romans 13:11-14)

This passage of Scripture shows us seven elements of the life of a prophetic people. These are seven signs of a people who know the time.

1. They Will Be Spiritually Awake.

"It is high time to awake out of sleep." They will not be asleep spiritually. They will be aware of the day and the hour in which they live.

The enemy is committed to putting the church to sleep. He wants to put us to sleep by ignorance; by a lack of understanding and a lack of knowledge of the ways of the Lord. In this way God's people will be destroyed. A prophetic people will know the time and will stay awake spiritually.

2. They Will Live a Holy and Clean Life.

"Let us therefore cast off the works of darkness." A prophetic people do not become trapped in the snare of the world. When they are spiritually awake they will be able to live a holy and clean life.

3. They Will Have Great Motivation to Be Involved in the Work of the Kingdom of God.

"Let us put on the armour of light." They will be on the front lines, ready to go to war in the Lord's army. People with no prophetic awareness of the times do not realize that the church is engaged in a great spiritual struggle. Those who are just floundering around cannot have any real motivation to participate in the work of the kingdom. Those who do know the time will be motivated and involved with an eternal, kingdom perspective.

4. They Will Live a Transparent, Open, and Honest Life.

"Let us walk honestly, as in the day." If they are spiritually aware of who they are, what their mission is and where they are going, they do not need to have a facade. They will be able to walk openly and confidently before God and man.

5. They Will Avoid Carnal Living.

"Not in rioting and drunkenness, not in clambering and wantonness, not in strife and envying." They will not become caught up in their own carnal appetites. Because they have a true prophetic understanding of the times and strategies of the enemy, they will clearly see the enemy's traps and be able to avoid them.

6. They Will Lean Totally Upon Jesus.

"But put ye on the Lord Jesus Christ." They will be ever aware of the presence of the Lord in their lives (past, present, and future) and in their ministries.

In order to walk with prophetic insight they must be able to look back and say, "If it had not been for the Lord, where would I be today?" The awareness of the times they have already lived through will make them more aware of the need to totally lean on Him in the future. They will trust Him and He will be able to lead them into all He has planned for their lives.

7. They Will Keep Their Priorities in Order.

"And make not provision for the flesh, to fulfil the lusts thereof." If they know the time and have prophetic understanding concerning the purposes of God for their lives, they will be able to keep their priorities in order. They will seek the kingdom of God first and make it the center of their lives and work. In that way all of God's purposes can be realized in their lives.

If we remove the prophetic dimension from our lives, the opposite of these seven things will tend to be present. We will go to sleep spiritually and not be aware of the time in which we live.

We will tend to live an unholy and unclean life. The things of this world will easily contaminate our lives. We will not be very motivated to devote our life to the work of the kingdom of God. We may be involved in a lot of things but all for selfish reasons.

We will tend to live a life of hypocrisy. We may attend church regularly and do all the things required of faithful members. But not being aware of the times, our spiritual lives will tend to be shallow and superficial. We will often be just going through the motions, doing what everyone else is doing, focusing only on what is expected of us.

We will tend to be controlled by our fleshly desires. Without an eternal, kingdom perspective, temporal, worldly pleasures will be so attractive to us that we will find it very difficult to resist them.

We will tend to walk independently from God. When Peter attempted to serve the Lord without leaning entirely on Him, he failed to understand the words of Jesus and therefore was not able to respond rightly. In three days Jesus was going to rise from the dead and be forever triumphant. But Peter had no prophetic insight into the words and actions of Jesus and consequently betrayed his Lord.

Lastly, our priorities will tend to be out of order. If we are unaware of the meaning of our lives and the times in which we live, how can we properly order the priorities of our lives?

TIMES OF TESTING

Sometimes the Lord will allow there to be a lull in the prophetic anointing. He will hold off speaking for a time to see how deep our commitment is to the spiritual word He has been speaking. When the tide is out it is reveals how much debris there is on the beach. So when there is a pause in the prophetic, we are often exposed for what we really are.

Are we a prophetic people or not? How well have we received the prophetic word? Have we merely let it scintillate us, excite us, give us goose bumps? Or have we prayed and labored over it to bring it to pass in our lives? Have we mixed it with faith and held on to it, even during the dark times when it does not seem like there is any hope for fulfillment. Have we lived loosely and trifled with the word that was spoken to us when the anointing was heavy?

"Let us therefore fear, lest, a promise (a prophetic word) being left us of entering into His rest, any of you should seem to come short of it. For unto us was the gospel preached, as well as unto them;

but the (prophetic) word preached did not profit them, not being mixed with faith in them that heard it." (Hebrews 4:1-2, additions mine)

The gap of silence that the Lord tests us with will reveal if we are truly a prophetic people. Those are not times to panic, but to evaluate what we have done with God's revealed word to us.

EARS TO HEAR

Just as the Lord deals with individuals in unique ways, and gives them different directives through the prophetic word, so the Lord deals with every church and congregation in personal, unique ways. He is revealing His plans to churches, but He does not always give the same word to each one.

This principle is brought out in the first three chapters of Revelation. In Revelation 1:18-19 our Lord declares, *"I am He that liveth, and was dead; and, behold, I am alive for evermore, Amen; and have the keys of hell and death. Write the things which thou has seen, and the things which are, and the things which shall be hereafter."*

John was commanded to write about things that have been, that are, and that shall be. Knowing those things marked him as a prophetic person. Knowing where we have been, where we are, and where we are going also marks a congregation as a prophetic people.

In Revelation 2 and 3 the Lord spoke to each church: to the church at Ephesus (2:1), at Smyrna (2:8), at Pergamos (2:12), at Thyatira (2:18), at Sardis (3:1), at Philadelphia (3:7), and at Laodicea (3:14). The Lord wanted each of the seven churches to understand the things that they had seen, which they were seeing, and which they were to see in the future. He wanted them to have prophetic understanding.

Each church received a different message. Even though they were living at the same time; even though the church as a whole may have been experiencing similar things, each church received special instructions from the Lord. Each one had to hear what the Lord was saying to them so they could respond in obedience.

Today, the Lord is also saying something different to each church. We cannot just pick up the word from another church. We cannot just join the bandwagon of another congregation. Each church must be listening to the voice of the Spirit for itself. It must have ears to hear what the Spirit is saying to them as a unique congregation.

The Lord does have something He wants to say to each of us as a prophetic people. Each congregation needs to be listening to His voice. The Lord wants to adjust us so we can be overcomers in our generation. And to be overcomers we need to have the prophetic word in our midst. Over and over again the cry of the Holy Spirit to the seven churches of Asia was, *"He that hath an ear, let him hear what the Spirit saith unto the churches"* (Revelation 2:7, 11, 17, 29; 3:6, 13, 22).

May we all ask for grace to have ears to hear what God is specifically saying to each of our congregations. Let us ask for grace to obey all the Lord has already spoken to us. May we seek His mercy to mix faith with all prophetic words that will come to us in the future.

Because we are a prophetic people who know where we are going and how we are going to get there, present negative circumstances will not slow us down in our service in the Kingdom. The Lord will continue to give us clear prophetic direction and we will be ready to follow the Lord wherever He might lead us.

We are positioning ourselves to continually hear the Word of the Lord. Our part is to make sure we stay alert and keep our ears open to hear what the Spirit is saying.

PROPHETIC PRINCIPLE

Why do some local churches have a prophetic spirit in their midst and others do not? What would keep us from being a prophetic people? How can we make sure that we as a church have an ear to hear what the Spirit is saying to us?

1. Have a Prophetic Vision for Your City.

I firmly believe that our attitude toward our city will profoundly affect our spiritual hearing ability. If we want to have a clear understanding of what the Lord is saying to the church, we must see our city in the way the Lord sees it.

The Scriptures have much to say about cities and communities. The Lord is concerned about and committed to reaching cities. Through the years I have consistently found that pastors who have a negative attitude toward their city, those who have no progressive vision for what the Lord wants to do in their city, are missing the dynamic prophetic spirit in their local church. The fact that they have no prophetic vision for their city implies that there is no prophetic insight in the church.

Abraham had a prophetic attitude toward Sodom, so before the Lord judged the city He talked with Abraham about it. Abraham's attitude could have been, "Go ahead and destroy it, I hate that city." If that had been his attitude, God would not have discussed it with him. Instead, Abraham pleaded for the city and interceded with God on behalf of the city. Because Abraham was the friend of God and had God's heart toward people and cities, God could count on his having the right attitude. As a result of his attitude, Abraham was able to hear what the Lord's thoughts were regarding Sodom.

On the other hand, Jonah did not have the same kind of attitude toward Nineveh. In fact, Jonah hated Nineveh and refused to preach in that city. He hated the people, the sin, and the crimes the Assyrians had perpetrated against his own people. The Lord told Jonah to preach in Nineveh but he tried every way he could to keep from it. Finally, God sent a big fish to transport him there and he was forced to preach God's Word to the city. As a result, the whole city repented and turned to the Lord. This was one of the greatest revivals in history. A city of 600,000 inhabitants turned to the Lord and committed themselves to Him. Jonah ran because He realized God was merciful and would forgive the people if they repented. He understood God's heart for the city.

Jesus demonstrated the right attitude toward Jerusalem. Even though He knew He was to be crucified in that city, when they rejected Him, He wept over the city. That word "wept" does not mean that Jesus became kind of sad and teary-eyed. It means that He sobbed over the city. He had great compassion for Jerusalem, the very compassion of His Father. He said, *"O Jerusalem, Jerusalem, thou that killest the prophets, and stonest them which are sent unto thee, how often would I have gathered thy children together, even as a hen gathereth her chickens under her wings, and ye would not"* (Matthew 23:37). They had missed their day of visitation and Jesus wept over them. He could have said, "Because you have rejected me, I am going to cast you off." But that was not what was in His heart. He loved His city.

That must also be our attitude toward our city. No matter how much crime, violence, and corruption it may have, we must have God's own heart of love for our city and the people in the city. God places us in cities to love and care for them, to be light and salt in the city. He wants us to reach out to the people in love. He wants us to reach out to the city government, pray for them and strengthen them. He wants us to be a part of the solution to the problems plaguing the city. But if we do not love our city, it will be impossible for us to be a dynamic prophetic presence in the city. If we have a negative attitude toward our city, we are not going to be able to reach it. God will not be able to speak to us and direct us concerning His plans for the people in that city.

2. Have a Prophetic Vision for Your Local Church.

The Bible refers to the local church as the city of God: *"But ye are come unto mount Sion, and unto the city of the living God, the heavenly Jerusalem, and to an innumerable company of angels, to the general assembly and church of the firstborn"* (Hebrews 12:22-23). Our attitude toward the local church will also have a profound impact on whether or not we have ears to hear what the Spirit is saying to the church.

Our attitude towards the city of God determines our ability to hear the voice of the Lord. The voice of the Lord may come to the church through anyone, and if there is strife and division in the church, the voice of the Lord will simply not be heard. Satan knows that and seeks to cause division as his primary method of removing the hearing ear from the church. The call of the Spirit for unity in the body of Christ today has a greater purpose than teaching us to love one another more fully. Our unity will also enable us to hear the voice of the Lord more fully, give the church ears to hear, and as a result, the church will be strong, bear fruit, and will not miss whatever the Lord purposes for it. If we have a wrong attitude toward the church, if we do not take care of personal offenses the biblical way, we will soon become deaf to the spirit of prophecy and will lose our bearings as a prophetic people.

It is so easy for something in our spirit to come between us and our ability to hear God's voice. That is why Jesus said, *"if thou bring thy gift to the altar, and there rememberest that thy brother hath ought against thee; leave there thy gift before the altar, and go thy way; first be reconciled to thy brother, and then come and offer thy gift"* (Matthew 5:23-24). Jesus says, "Before I can communicate with you, you must go and clear up any offenses you might have with your brother. Until then, I can not clearly direct your lives." We cannot hear the Lord's voice if offenses are dividing us.

THE CHURCH IS THE CITY OF GOD

What are the attitudes we are to have toward the city of God? Primarily we are to address the problems of the church with compassion, prayer, and faith in God. Hatred, fault-finding, fear and unbelief, pride—these are the kinds of attitudes that will block the leading of the Holy Spirit in the church.

That does not mean we are to be blind to the problems and needs in the church. It simply means that when we face needs, we pray rather than criticize. We encourage and lift up rather than tear down. We reach out and restore rather than bury with contempt. We will do this if we remember that the city is the Lord's! The house of God is the Lord's! Our job is to have God's attitude toward His house, and to allow Him to succeed in His purposes for His house without our taking any of the credit for it.

Nehemiah exemplified the right kind of attitude toward the city of God in his attitude toward Jerusalem.

"So I came to Jerusalem, and was there three days. And I arose in the night, I and some men with me; neither told I any man what my God had put in my heart to do at Jerusalem: neither was there any beast with me, save the beast that I rode upon. And I went out by night by the gate of the valley, even before the dragon well, and to the dung port, and viewed the walls of Jerusalem, which were broken down, and the gates thereof were consumed with fire. . . . Then said I unto them, 'Ye see the distress that we are in, how Jerusalem lieth waste, and the gates thereof are burned with fire: come, and let us build up the wall of Jerusalem, that we be no more a reproach.' Then I told them of the hand of my God which was good upon me; as also the king's words that he had spoken unto me. And they said, 'Let us rise up and build.' So they strengthened their hands for this good work. But when Sanballat

the Horonite, and Tobiah the servant, the Ammonite, and Geshem the Arabian, heard it, they laughed us to scorn, and despised us, and said, 'What is this thing that ye do? Will ye rebel against the king?' Then answered I them, and said unto them, 'The God of heaven, he will prosper us; therefore we his servants will arise and build: but ye have no portion, nor right, nor memorial in Jerusalem.'" (Nehemiah 2:11-13, 17-20)

Here was a man of God with a vision for his city. The city was in ruins. The walls had crumbled, the gates had been burned, the city was filled with rubbish. But what did Nehemiah see? He saw what God saw! That was the important thing.

To have a prophetic vision means that we see the house of the Lord the way God sees it. Some may say that is not being realistic, but I believe Nehemiah was being realistic. He fully appreciated the problems facing him in Jerusalem but he also saw God's solution. He was hearing God's plans. He saw a glorious city with restored walls and the presence of Almighty God in their midst. His head was not in the sand. He saw the real condition of the city. But he also had eyes to see and ears to hear from God's prophetic viewpoint.

If all we see is what we are able to see with our natural eyes, we will not be able to have a prophetic vision for the house. Eventually we will just be tempted to quit. Nehemiah had a word from God. He knew what the Lord had planned for the city. He waited for God's voice, received a strategy from the Lord, and went to work. He knew the Lord was going to make the city glorious and he wanted to be part of the solution rather than part of the problem.

God wants to touch our cities. He wants to make our churches a light that shines on a hill over the city. That is His plan. But what do we see? Sure, we have problems. If we hear the voice of the Lord and follow His leadership, even though we are not perfect, we know we are going in the right direction. The Lord is restoring His church and will continue to do so until He has fulfilled all His purposes for it. But we can only see that if we see what God sees. That is the spirit of prophecy and that is what keeps us going in the right direction.

If we do not have that spirit, we will be easily distracted by all of the blemishes and problems we see around us. We will not see a glorious church, we will only see desolation and end up feeling despair.

Here is how the Lord sees the church:

"Look upon Zion, the city of our solemnities: thine eyes shall see Jerusalem a quiet habitation, a tabernacle that shall not be taken down; not one of the stakes thereof shall ever be removed, neither shall any of the cords thereof be broken. But there the glorious Lord will be unto us a place of broad rivers and streams; wherein shall go no galley with oars, neither shall gallant ship pass thereby. For the Lord is our judge, the Lord is our lawgiver, the Lord is our king; he will save us." (Isaiah 33:20-21)

Jerusalem is not going to be a place where the ships of war come in and blast away. Peace will be in the streets of the city of God. Where the Lord is there will be broad rivers and streams bringing life to the people. The Lord will be the Judge and King of His city.

What do you see when you look at the church? Have your spiritual ears been plugged by pride, criticism, fear, and unbelief? Is unforgiveness keeping you from hearing what the Spirit is saying? If so, turn to the Lord with all your heart. Ask the Lord for fresh vision. Ask Him for a heart of compassion. Ask Him to show you what He sees and to make you a dynamic part of His kingdom purposes. The Lord wants us to be a prophetic people. He wants us to be a people who know who we are, where we have come from, and where we are going. Let us allow the Lord to open our ears and make us a prophetic people in our generation.

CHAPTER TEN

Successful Truth:
True Prosperity

Money tests people—it brings out the best and the worst in them. Material blessing either humbles them or makes them proud. Money forces people to choose what they will do with it. A prosperous person can humble himself, recognize his dependence on God, and invest his abundance in things of eternal value. Or, he can inflate his own ego, spend money on himself, hoard for his retirement, and let covetousness control him.

The Scriptures contain many warnings about covetousness. To covet is the very root of mankind's problem. The Lord gives a key warning to us in Luke 12:15, *"for a man's life consisteth not in the abundance of the things which he possesseth."*

THE PROBLEM OF COVETOUSNESS

Starting with the first sin in the Garden of Eden, right up to our own day, the central root sin of mankind has always been covetousness.

- Eve desired to be like God. She coveted His knowledge, His position. *I will be like God if I take and eat of this fruit,* she thought. Her sin spread death to all of mankind.

- Lot's wife looked back at Sodom because she coveted her lifestyle there, and for doing so died on the spot.

- Achan took the forbidden spoils of war and hid them in his tent. It cost him his life and the lives of his family.

- David coveted his neighbor's wife. It brought ruin to his family and even to the whole nation.

In all of these examples, we see that covetousness is at the heart of the human problem. No wonder the conclusion and summary of the Ten Commandments is *"Thou shalt not covet"* (Exodus 20:17).

The word covet means "a craving, a desire for more, greediness, a dissatisfaction with what is enough, never satisfied, and a desire to have what is another's." In other words, it is a "give me-me-me" spirit. It is a desire of the human soul that finds fulfillment in many things, but never in God.

It is very easy for us to respond with covetousness. That is obviously why the Bible talks about it so much. The Tenth Commandment is, *"Thou shalt not covet"* (Exodus 20:17)–all of the preceding nine have covetousness as their root. It is as though the Lord were saying, "If you could overcome a covetous spirit, you would not break any of the Lord's commandments."

God knows all about the necessities of life. He knows what we need better than we do. He also loves to bless us with abundance. But when blessings come our way, it is an opportunity for us to take spiritual inventory of our lives. It is an opportunity to review our values and the things that really are important in our lives. God is not against blessings or prosperity. God is not against us having material things. But He does not want things to control us.

Whenever we are blessed, either we will see God's love or we will see our abilities. When we receive material blessings, our response needs to be filled with a sense of gratitude. From that, we can learn to understand God's purpose for blessing us.

THE PURPOSE FOR PROSPERITY

God knows covetousness can destroy us. That is why it is so important we clearly understand God's view of prosperity. Paul's gives us God's view when he writes to Timothy, *"Charge them that are rich in this world, that they be not highminded . . ."* (1 Timothy 6:17a). The first word of instruction is "Do not be filled with pride." Pride and self-centeredness is the essence of sin. Pride always perverts the blessings of the Lord.

Paul goes on further to say, *". . . nor trust in uncertain riches, but in the living God, who giveth us richly all things to enjoy"* (1 Timothy 6:17b).

God is the One who gives us all things to enjoy. Nothing is wrong with enjoying the blessings of the Lord, but covetousness is a serious problem. Pride, self-centeredness, self-satisfaction, and self-sufficiency twist God's blessings. If we are proud of our things, it will not be long until we begin to trust in them and to find our satisfaction and identity in them. For blessings not to become a curse we must maintain our dependence on the Lord. Thus, Paul's second word to us is that we must trust in the Lord alone.

God fills people's barns to enable them to do good; to accomplish good things that would not be possible if they did not have an abundance. *"Let them [be]. . .ready to give, willing to share"* (1 Timothy 6:18).

Paul's third exhortation to the rich believers is that they be governed by generosity in all things. The Lord placed them in a position to give. When blessings come their way they are to be immediately ready to give and willing to share with others less fortunate than themselves. *". . . Laying up in store for themselves a good foundation against the time to come"* (1 Timothy 6:19).

Godly men and women who have been blessed with an abundance see those blessings from a different perspective. They understand that they are investing in the future, even the far-distant future, *". . . that they may lay hold on eternal life."* (1 Timothy 6:19)

Whether rich or poor, believers are to think, value, and judge from an eternal perspective. We must understand that we are not going to be here forever. Material things around us are temporary. They are all secondary to the eternal. The values of believers are to be derived from the eternal, not from the temporal.

When Paul refers to uncertain riches he means that money and material things come and go. I can hear some say, "Well, I have never had to worry about them coming my way!" But they may! Uncertain riches have a way of showing up when you least expect them. Some rich uncle could die and give you a large amount of money. Then what would you do?

What happens to people when prosperity sweeps in on them? I have personally watched this happen. I have seen it bring the best out of people. I have seen people use their wealth to bless, to share, to give, to reach out—to help others. And I have seen it bring the worst out of people. In fact, recent studies suggest that approximately one-third of all lottery winners must eventually file for bankruptcy. Prosperity can either bless or destroy someone, the outcome is based on the prosperous person's maturity.

PROSPERITY AND MATURITY

Some people believe and might suggest that material blessings are a sign that we are really spiritual. If we are rich, it is because God considers us to be a special person in His kingdom. He has given us all these things because of the maturity of our faith. Nothing could be further from the truth! Nothing could be less biblical!

One of the most important things for us to clearly understand is that things—money and material things—are not any kind of a measure of a person's worthiness or spirituality. And neither is poverty. What makes a believer spiritually mature is how they handle riches.

When Peter suddenly received a great abundance of fish, what was his response? How did his wealth affect him? His boats were full. God had poured out tremendous wealth upon him. He had such an abundance there was more than enough for himself and the other boats around him. He could have said, "Now I can finally live like a wealthy fisherman! My neighbors will finally see how successful and important I really am!" Instead of that, Peter said, *"Depart from me, for I am a sinful man, O Lord!"* (Luke 5:8). He humbled himself because he felt he was not worthy to be in God's presence. The blessings of God should make us humble, not cocky, haughty, or proud.

How did Jacob respond when he was so bountifully blessed? Did he say, "I deserve all this wealth. It was my cleverness that has resulted in all this. Look at what I have accomplished!" He said, *"I am not worthy of the least of all the mercies, and of all the truth, which thou hast shewed unto thy servant"* (Genesis 32:10).

King David was magnificently blessed. He had more power, influence, and wealth than anyone in his kingdom. He could have easily taken credit for his accomplishments. Instead he said, *"But who am I, and what is my people. . .for all things come of thee"* (1 Chronicles 29:14). David exemplified an attitude of true humility.

A person's maturity is discovered by their response to blessing. Those who are mature are humbled and intend to bless others with their prosperity. Those who are not mature become proud and haughty—and attempt to keep the blessing to themselves. When blessings come, we have a choice of how we respond. Either we bless ourselves or we reach out and bless others.

WINDOWS OR MIRRORS

Like one-way glass, material blessings can be either a window or a mirror. One-way glass surrounds my office. From one side, it is a mirror. From the other side it is a window. If I am on the inside, I can see out. From that vantage-point it is a window. However, when I walk outside I can no longer see through the glass—all I can see is my own reflection. From that perspective it is a mirror. The same glass is a window on one side and a mirror on the other.

Material blessings may function in our lives like mirrors. All we can see is how to bless ourselves. Or they will be like a window—a window of opportunity to share with others. The decision is ours. Our approach to these blessings reveals what is in our hearts.

Moses warned the new nation of Israel about responding properly to material blessings of the Lord.

"And it shall be, when the Lord thy God shall have brought thee into the land which he sware unto thy fathers, to Abraham, to Isaac, and to Jacob, to give thee great and goodly cities, which thou buildedst not, and houses full of all good things, which thou filledst not, and wells digged, which thou diggedst not, vineyards and olive trees, which thou plantedst not; when thou shalt have eaten and be full; then beware lest thou forget the Lord, which brought thee forth out of the land of Egypt, from the house of bondage." (Deuteronomy 6:10-12)

The Lord is concerned about us. He knows money and material things have the potential to bring out either the best or the worst in us. Such blessings either will inflate our egos, or they will humble us and enable us to see God.

ENJOYMENT OR ENLARGEMENT

A self-centered person uses the blessings of the Lord for his personal enjoyment only. A godly person will look for an opportunity to invest in something greater than himself. He will want to see those blessings enlarged to accomplish the will of God. He will look for a chance to reach out and share, to help and minister to others.

The Lord may richly give us all things to enjoy. But when we ignore God and the needs of our brothers and sisters, we certainly do not manage the Lord's resources according to the Lord's will.

If a Christian father suddenly heard from his employer that he had been given a major promotion and a large bonus, he would be very anxious to get back to his family and share the good news and the bonus with them. His first thought would be to bless his family. He would think of how he could meet needs he was unable to meet in the past.

A selfish father would think only of himself. "Well, now I can finally join the country club. I am going to be able buy that boat I have always wanted. I am really going to have some fun!" His approach reveals sin in the heart of man. If we really want to use the blessings of the Lord according to the ways of the Lord, then we must invest them in others so that we can experience true enlargement.

We can take three approaches to life:

1. We Can Waste Our Lives Like the Prodigal Son.

We can receive abundance from the Lord and use it up on our own enjoyment.

2. We Can Hoard It Like the Elder Brother.

He stayed home and piled up goods higher and higher until he could not see anything else. When his long-lost brother returned home all he saw was a threat to his hoard.

3. We Can Invest It.

We can give it away so that it will bring new life. That is what God Himself does with His life. And that is what He wants us to do. He wants us to invest His bountiful blessings into the lives of others.

The Lord gives a certain amount of goods and a limited amount of time to accomplish His will. Hoarding blessings will never achieve the purpose of God. The Lord gives to us so that we can give to others in need. We need to wisely bless others while we are living. Our children will not need help when they are 50 and we are 80. They need help now. Now is the time to invest in those we love. We need to invest wisely to help and serve others.

The missionary who gave his life for the Gospel in Ecuador, Jim Elliott, wrote, "He is no fool who gives what he cannot keep to gain what he cannot lose."

WORRY OR TRUST

The reason covetousness takes hold of a man is that he has little faith or trust in God for the future. A rich farmer who built bigger and better barns to hoard his goods must have been plagued with worry.

> "The sleep of a laboring man is sweet, whether he eats little or much; but the abundance of the rich will not suffer him to sleep."
> (Ecclesiastes 5:12)

Money and material things do not bring peace. If we trust in things instead of God, we will not have peace. Instead, we will have continual worry and ultimate frustration. Worry proves that we have not trusted in God for our blessings. Worry is not reasonable, natural, useful, necessary, or spiritual.

1. Not Reasonable

"The life is more than meat, and the body is more than raiment."
(Luke 12:23)

Life goes far beyond things. It is unreasonable to focus on the amount of material goods we have when life has so much more eternal significance.

2. Not Natural

"Consider the ravens: for they neither sow nor reap, which neither have storehouse nor barn; and God feedeth them: how much more are ye better than the fowls?" (Luke 12:24)

Anyone can see that God faithfully provides for the needs of other creatures. And anyone can see that God has created man to be the pinnacle of His creation. Why worry?

"Consider the lilies how they grow: they toil not, they spin not; and yet I say unto you, that Solomon in all his glory was not arrayed like one of these." (Luke 12:27)

God never designed us to worry. When we give in to unbelief and worry, it will prove to be very costly.

3. Not Useful

"And which of you with taking thought can add to his stature one cubit? If ye then be not able to do that thing which is least, why take ye thought for the rest?" (Luke 12:25-26)

The reason we worry and get caught up in covetousness is that we want to protect ourselves. We want to eliminate any need for further worry. We want to make our lives safe and secure through our own means and resources. But the very opposite happens. When we determine to look out for ourselves, to run our own lives for our own benefit, we only increase our worry. Then we have to worry about losing things. We have to worry about what might lay in the future that could foil our well-laid plans.

We have got to trust God at all times; when we have enough or when we do not. All else is greed and frustration.

4. Not Necessary

"If then God so clothe the grass, which is today in the field, and tomorrow is cast into the oven; how much more will he clothe you, O ye of little faith?" (Luke 12:28)

It is so easy to pick up a spirit of worry. When times are tough, it is natural to see life through negative, dark glasses and fret about everything. Yet the Lord has committed Himself to caring for us at all times.

5. Not Spiritual

"And seek not ye what ye shall eat, or what ye shall drink, neither be ye of doubtful mind." (Luke 12:29)

A worrying mind is a carnal mind. Worry comes from unbelief, not faith.

So what is the cure for worry? STOP LIVING FOR THINGS! Do not make the accumulation of wealth and material things the goal of life. When they come to you, enjoy them, but do not live for them. LIVE FOR GOD!

WISE LIVING

Solomon was known as the wisest man on earth. He learned this lesson as no one else has. The wise man concluded that things come and go. None of them are eternal. They all are vanity, empty, meaningless. A life spent pursuing them is meaningless.

"I made me great works; I builded me houses; I planted me vineyards: I made me gardens and orchards, and I planted trees in them of all kind of fruits: I made me pools of water, to water therewith the wood that bringeth forth trees: I got me servants and maidens, and had servants born in my house; also I had great possessions of great and small cattle above all that were in Jerusalem before me: I gathered me also silver and gold, and the peculiar treasure of kings and of the provinces: I gat me men singers and women singers, and the delights of the sons of men, as musical instruments, and that of all sorts. So I was great, and increased more than all that were before me in Jerusalem: also my wisdom remained with me. And whatsoever mine eyes desired I kept not from them, I withheld not my heart from any joy; for my heart rejoiced in all my labour: and this was my portion of all my labour. Then I looked on all the works that my hands had wrought, and on the labour that I had laboured to do: and, behold, all was vanity and vexation of spirit, and there was no profit under the sun." (Ecclesiastes 2:4-11)

Next he tried to find meaning in life in human reason alone. He started his search with material things. Then he searched his own mind and he ended with emptiness in his soul. He turned to philosophies. He searched and searched. *"And I turned myself to consider wisdom, and madness, and folly. . . this also is vanity"* (Ecclesiastes 2:12,15).

So is there no meaning in life? Is there no escape from the cycle of vanity, worry, and anxiety? In the end Solomon answered, Yes. God has a way to avoid a wasted life. God has a way to overcome covetousness. The true meaning of this life can be simply summed up.

"Let us hear the conclusion of the whole matter: Fear God and keep His commandments, for this is the whole duty of man. For God shall bring every work into judgment, with every secret thing, whether it be good or whether it be evil." (Ecclesiastes 12:13-14)

This is the whole duty of man, the whole meaning of a man's life. First, we are to fear God. We are to have an awesome reverence and respect for God, for His nature and His power. We are to take God and His will into consideration in every situation. We are to live our lives knowing that God loves and cares for us. We are never to forget that we will always have necessary things. The Lord has promised to provide for our every need.

Second, we are to keep the Lord's commandments. We are to live according to God's Word. The absolute standards and revealed truths of the Scriptures are to be our constant guide through life.

A lot of people today think, "If I just had more, my soul would be satisfied. If I could rise to a certain level in society, I would be satisfied." But the Bible clearly teaches power and wealth will not satisfy. No temporary things will ever satisfy the human soul.

WHO DO WE TRUST?

Understand clearly, it is not sinful for us to have money and material things. It is not sinful for us to provide for the future. It is not sinful for us to enjoy the things we have. But it is sinful when we depend upon them and not upon the Lord.

When we stop worrying about possessions, that is a sign we fear God. Possessions are given to us to be used in God's kingdom. We cannot bless others unless we first receive from the Lord. But the moment those possessions are looked upon as being for us alone, we are out of step with the will of God.

When God opens the storehouse of His blessings, they are designed to bless others, and in this way, to glorify His name. For the rich fool in Luke 12, the blessings of the Lord were a mirror, not a window. All he could see was himself and his desires. When he looked at all his goods, he was unable to see others and their needs. And so God said to this man, *"Thou fool!"* (Luke 12:20). He was a fool to think the substance in his barn was the essence of his life. We are fools to think we could find true satisfaction in things. Riches are uncertain at best. They come and they go. They are temporary. They have no eternal meaning in and of themselves.

This temporary mode of existence could end at any moment. Then what will we do, since we have devoted this life to temporal things? To the rich fool, Jesus said, *"this night thy soul shall be required of thee: then whose shall those things be, which thou hast provided?"* (Luke 12:20).

We cannot take any of these things with us. This life is given to us for the purpose of investing in eternity. If we invest only in this age, what will we do when we come to the end of our lives? *"For we brought nothing into this world, and it is certain we can carry nothing out."* (1 Timothy 6:7).

Even if we have descendants who will inherit our goods, will they last forever? All our goods can do is rust, decay, and disintegrate.

In this life only people's souls are eternal. We should use our temporal material goods to invest in people's lives. Invest in our families. Invest in our brothers and sisters in the body of Christ. We must use the blessings God has given us to help others. We are in this life for that one purpose. Life is truly life only when it is poured out to others.

That shows the love of God. That demonstrates the glory of God. That is what gives our lives true meaning.

What if you are a believer in Jesus Christ and you now realize that money, things, and a concern for them have gained a measure of control over your life? It could happen to anyone. It happens to the rich and it happens to the poor. It is so easy to worry about how to get enough money, how to meet all your daily needs. You allow that spirit of worry, which is a spirit of unbelief, to come into your life. Soon you do not trust God to meet your needs and to be your satisfaction any more.

God wants you to depend on Him alone! Why? Because He alone is your Creator, life, and true satisfaction. If you stood before God today and He asked you, "What did you do with the things I gave you?" what would you say? "Well Lord I used them to help others. I blessed my family. I blessed the house of the Lord. I blessed the work of God. I put your kingdom and people first." Or, "Well Lord, I didn't know for sure if I was going to make it. So, I just kind of got wrapped up in myself and in my own needs. I was just trying to survive and make sure I had plenty for me. So I didn't really share it."

You do not know what the future holds. You do not know if you will ever have as much money as you think you need. So where are you going to put your hope? What are you going to depend on? Where will your confidence be?

If you put your trust in God alone for the future and invest the blessings of the Lord wisely, your future will be secure in the hands of the Lord. He has promised to take care of you!

When you give yourself completely to the Lord, when He is in absolute control of your life, worry is obsolete. He will take care of you. You can trust Him! If you lose your job, you do not have to worry. Take a position of faith. Say, "I am going to depend on God for my future. If He gives me that new, higher paying job I'll use the extra money wisely. If He doesn't, I know the Lord will still provide!"

Make sure the spirit of covetousness does not take hold of you. Do not settle for a self-centered existence. Do not try to find satisfaction in a life full of things with emptiness of soul. Let your life be filled with God. Adopt a faith attitude toward life. Live according to God's wisdom regarding money and material things. Then and only then will you know true satisfaction, true life! Make Jesus the centerpiece of your life and set your heart to trust in Him alone. This is the true prosperity message.

CHAPTER ELEVEN

Dynamic Truth:
Releasing Real Spiritual Power

We all, ministers and congregations, want to be part of a dynamic church that is accomplishing the plan of God for our communities. We all want a church that is respected by society. Our deep desire is that the church be the church that God intended with all its purposes and glory manifested in every-day life.

But how is that accomplished? How is this brought about? How can we get God to breathe upon His body to bring it to a healthy life, strengthened by the awesome inner working of the Holy Spirit in every fiber of its being?

MANIFESTATIONS?

Whenever God blesses a congregation it is because He wants to accomplish something—it is for a purpose. After the people are healed and edified, He wants to accomplish His will in our communities. He wants His power demonstrated outside the four walls of our buildings. He wants His glory known throughout the earth.

God wants to touch the world with His glorious Gospel. He is concerned about winning the sinners to Christ. He wants His church to be glorious in the eyes of the world. He does not want His body taken lightly and mocked or misunderstood.

MIRACLES?

I was raised in American Pentecostal churches. When my parents went nightly to the revivals I remember dozing off on the hard benches until the meeting was over. Those on-going meetings were our life. We went to Assembly of God, Foursquare, and Pentecostal Church of God services. I was exposed to several different Pentecostal denominations, as well as independent churches.

T.L. Osborne was my pastor when I was a teenager. I later traveled with Gordon Lindsay for a short time. I knew some of the main healers of that day, like William Branham, Jack Cole, A.A. Allen, and some of the lesser known. I went to the great crusades of Oral Roberts where thousands of people flocked. People were drawn to all of these preachers because of the miracles and healing that occurred.

When I began holding meetings in nations outside America, people would come because of the miracles they heard were taking place. If you had asked me then what it was going to take to shake that region and turn everyone to God, I would have said, "more miracles!" I would have given you a convincing argument why that had to happen.

I am sure that many people were affected by the healing. Many were blessed by the miracles. But I have seen men of faith come and go. I have seen revivals come and go. I have seen revival meetings open and close. Looking back on it all, I do not think everything was accomplished that God desired for His church.

In fact, take a look at Jesus Christ's ministry on earth. For three and a half years he worked many miracles and healings in Israel. He pulled in the crowds. He gained a great reputation as a miracle worker. There was no limitation to his miracles: lepers were cleansed, blind eyes were opened, deaf ears were made whole, and even the dead were raised up! Right there in the busy streets, people witnessed the miracle-working power of Jesus. Thousands gathered. He even fed them miraculously when he finished teaching them! Everyone knew about Him.

But notice the results. The people only showed up for the miracles. There was no deep lasting effect in their hearts. They liked the good taste of the bread and fishes Jesus provided. The crowds were still fickle and whimsical. They came and went depending on if the teaching shaved them too close or not.

Something was missing. Experiencing miracles and the supernatural did not turn the people into a glorious congregation of the Lord. Miracles in themselves did not provide a means for turning them into a glorious church. They still did not have a concept of what the church should be like.

GREAT CRUSADES?

Is the answer to having a glorious church simply having great evangelistic crusades? Is that what is going to transform societies? Are concerted efforts of united local churches in a massive evangelism push the answer?

In our city we have had three major crusades by a leading, world-renown evangelist. They have been magnificent in bringing churches together for the crusades and thousands of people show up for the city-wide meetings. At the meetings there are many decisions for Christ made at the altar calls. But even his organization admits that a very small percentage of those decisions really last. They estimate that 95 percent of the harvest returns to where they were before the meetings began.

Jesus said He wanted fruit that remained (see John 15:16). I know we all would want a "quick fix" to society's problems, or an easy way to get people into the church. Sometimes we think, *Just hire an evangelist and get the city saved over night!* But that is not working. They bring in great crowds, but the crowds come and go. A transient crowd is not a "church family." It takes a stable church family, committed and dedicated, for God to transform a society.

TRANSFORMATION

God did transform the first disciples into a dynamic church. He established the kind of church that could turn the world upside-down. In Luke 24:49 we are told that Christ commanded the disciples to stay in Jerusalem until a unique event occurred. They were to stay until He transformed them into the dynamic move of God He intended to have as His witness in all the earth.

Ten days later, on the Day of Pentecost, all the members of the early church were baptized in the Holy Spirit! God dwelt in the believers in a new, powerful way. An explosion of power took place, as well as an explosion of understanding about the church. A major change took place in the hearts and mind of the disciples.

The Gospel went into all the world. It went from India and Africa to Spain and Britain. There were no airplanes, trains, printing presses, or radio, yet it exploded across the European and Asian continents.

THE ORIGINAL PATTERN

In that explosion of power and knowledge, God gave them a pattern for His church. The second chapter of Acts is the original pattern for the kind of church that reaches nations for God, affects societies, and transforms neighborhoods.

The first church that was established in the post-Pentecost outpouring is to be our pattern. We must use that pattern as a standard for our churches in each generation. In the twenty-first century, that has to be our standard as well. If we do not measure up to it, we need to change. Our church programs must align to that pattern.

CLASSIC CAR

Some years ago I got the desire to restore a classic car. I really like the 1957 Chevrolet Bellaire, two-door hard top, painted turquoise and ivory, with a turquois and black interior. If you are a car buff, you know that particular car is one of the classics of all the cars in the fifties. The only thing better would be a convertible—but it rains too much in Oregon where I live, for a convertible.

One day I saw in the newspaper, in the antique car section, just what I wanted: a half-restored 1957 car, off the frame restoration project! It was for sale! I picked up the phone and called, and my first question was whether or not the color was original. It must be the manufacturer's color to have real value. In fact, everything on the car must be like the original, or the antique value is lost.

I went over to his garage and saw this dismantled car that was turquoise, my favorite color! He had partially restored it starting with the basic main frame. Everything else was on the garage floor in boxes. There were twelve boxes full of parts. I got real excited about it and immediately bought it. But I did not know what I was getting into. There are ten thousand pieces to a 1957 Chevy two-door hardtop. I had thought it would only take a few weeks of work and I would have this car up and running.

Three winters later I still sat on the floor of my garage, freezing cold, working on it. I was scrubbing the little parts because every little piece had to be cleaned and then spray-painted with the original paint. There is a whole manual to follow, and every little part must be just like the original. If not, the value of the car drops. It has to be just like it was in the beginning.

One night a week, and some Saturdays, for three years, this went on, until we finally got it done. My son-in-law was the brains behind this project, and with his help it was finally done!

I remember well when it was finished. I got in behind the wheel and sat there for a moment. It was a neat feeling. It was beautiful because it was authentically restored, just like it was brand new. I turned the key on for a trial run. I had some friends in the back seat, and we started down the road.

ORIGINAL CHURCH

I have said all that to say this: if we are going to have the power of God released in the church, we must be restored to the original. We cannot say, "We do not need the fenders any more, we will just cut off the back. We will just adjust a little here, change some over there." We cannot say, "We will just change the church a little here, and make it different over there," and somehow the church will come out okay. If we are going to have a glorious church in action, releasing the power of God in its community, we must be like the original church.

1 Corinthians 3 very clearly states that Christ is the foundation of His House. It then admonishes us *"to take heed how [you] buildeth thereupon"* (1 Corinthians 3:10). We can build on it with cheap materials like wood, hay, and stubble if we want. Or we can build it out of gold, silver, and precious stone, just like the original blueprints called for. We can cut corners, thinking we are saving time or money, but it will not be like the original. It will not be as precious as the original and we will not save anything, after all. It will just be a cheap copy. Cheap materials will break down sooner, and we will have leaks, cracks, and slanted walls. When the storms come will have a mess on our hands.

But if we have built the House of God in the right way, with the original type of materials, it will stand when the storms of opposition come. We will be rewarded on Judgment Day for being a faithful workman and sticking to the original intent. That House will be a beacon in the community that releases the power of God.

THE BLUEPRINT

So, what did the original church look like? How was the original House built in the first place? Just like I had a picture of my car on the garage wall to look at so I'd restore it correctly, what picture of the church do we have? These are the questions I asked when I started pastoring at Bible Temple in the 1960s. "Lord, how was it in the beginning? Because that is the way I want to see the House built today."

As mentioned before, the answer was in the second chapter of Acts. The ingredients found there include repentance, water baptism, meeting together, reaching the community, releasing the power of God, and loving others. As we examine these ingredients, remember that this blueprint is to be followed today.

REPENTANCE

What is the first question people ask when God has pricked their consciences? They have recognized they are sinners, that the Messiah, Christ, has been crucified for their sins. They ask, "What shall we do?" Peter's response in Acts 2 was, *"Repent . . ."* (verse 38).

That comes first in a church wanting to release God's power. There must be genuine repentance by all people. If we do not understand repentance, we cannot really be saved. We often have an easy believism. We tell people to just raise their hand in response to our preaching, and we say, "I see that hand," as the piano plays softly in the background. There is no real repentance, and then we wonder why two weeks later they are back in sin and walking in darkness.

As chapter five states, repentance is a change of mind. A person must think differently about his sins. He must learn to think God's thoughts about his life. Whatever God says—that is what he should agree with and live by.

If we do not start with genuine repentance in the church, we are going to have a church full of religious people who are going nowhere in the kingdom of God, and who are not going to make an impact for good in society.

BAPTISM IN WATER

Peter went on in verse 38 to say *". . . and be baptized every one of you. . . ."* Water baptism is the next ingredient from the first church that is required of all churches today.

A new believer validates his faith by his obedience. If one says he is making Jesus Christ his Lord, the first step is that he show it by obedience to Him. That is shown by water baptism. Obedience in baptism is an identification with Jesus' death, burial, and resurrection. It is the forsaking (burial) of the old lifestyle, and the beginning (resurrection) of the new Christian life.

Ignoring water baptism is like forgetting the engine on the antique Chevy—it looks great but doesn't run too well. It is not the original pattern.

JOINED TOGETHER

"Then they that gladly received his word were baptized: and the same day there were added unto them about three thousand souls" (Acts 2:41). That word "added" is a key word. A new believer needs to be joined and placed into a family. Just as a newborn baby needs a family for nourishment, direction, teaching, and correction, it is important that a new Christian be part of a fellowship of believers.

"And they continued stedfastly in the apostles' doctrine. . ." (Acts 2:42). In Acts 2, the first church was into Bible study. Just as the apostles showed them how Christ fulfilled the Old Testament, we all need to be established in the facts of the faith. As they studied the basic principles of living in the Bible, so we must get into and interact with those principles to be successful in our lives. The original church was a teaching church.

Not only were the people joined together in the large corporate gathering, but they also fellowshiped in smaller units. *". . .and breaking bread from house to house. . ."* (Acts 2:46).

Each of these phrases exhibit the various ingredients of the original church. The corporate and smaller Bible studies were vital functions in the church. They were important then, and they are important today.

SOCIAL AGENCY

"And had all things common; and sold their possessions and goods, and parted them to all men, as every man had need" (Acts 2:44-45). Something had transpired in the souls of the early church members. Instead of being selfish, they started reaching out to others. This was not a forced communism but a change of heart that exuded compassion voluntarily. Their Christianity was very practical.

They began to ask, "What can I do to help people? What can I do to lift some loads? How can I help my fellow Christian? How can I serve my brother?" Service was the key word in the new Christian life. Jesus made that very clear in His teachings and in His actions. He felt comfortable taking a towel and washing His disciples' feet. It was no threat to His manhood, or to His Deity! He admonished us all to, in like manner, serve one another.

Love is not supposed to be just a noun, but a verb, in Christianity. We do not just say "Bless you, be on your way." Love denotes action. We do whatever we can to help each other on our journey. The church in Acts 2 made it important and today's church should also hold service in high regard.

RELEASING THE POWER

Beyond meeting the needs of the poor, elderly, widows, and orphans in the church, we must release the power of Christ in the world. This is important—and this is where many churches fail. Usually this failure is based on two misconceptions.

First, we tend to limit spiritual ministry to within the four walls of the church building. Often, the best-kept secret of the Gospel is its power to transform lives. We all have been guilty of putting its light under a bushel. But God wants the world to see His glory. A true church is one that manifests that glory to the world. It takes Christ to the street. It takes the Gospel to the neighborhood. The whole parable of the Good Samaritan was given in response to the question, *"Who is my neighbour?"* (Luke 10:29). The second greatest commandment is to love your *"neighbour as thyself"* (Luke 10:27). And Jesus taught that "the neighbor" is anyone in need. And we are to minister to them wherever we meet them.

The second misconception in our churches is that we tend to limit ministry to the "five-fold leadership" ministries. In a sense, we deify those five ministries: apostle, prophet, evangelist, pastor, and teacher (see Ephesians 4:11). We put up a line of demarcation between the clergy and the laity.

Sometimes it is the minister's fault. We often say that the greatest calling a young man can have is the call into the ministry. Meaning the preaching or pastoring ministry.

As a result of that type of thinking, that type of admonishing, many potential opportunities for ministry are lost. "If only I had settled down as a teen-ager, and not run about, and gone to Bible School, I could have been a minister in the church—and performed good for the Lord. But I have lost that chance, so I'll just sit in the pews the rest of my life."

God never planned it that way. He only uses the ministry for *"the perfecting of the saints, for the work of the ministry"* (Ephesians 4:12). He uses the leadership team to perfect the saints for the work of ministering. Some call this body ministry. Each member, joint, or part of the Body supplies a need. Each Christian has a unique contribution to the work of the ministry. Each member in the church is to be matured, developed, skilled in his own gifting, and is to then minister to the church, and to the world, under the blessing and anointing of God!

The power of God is to be released to the world through every member in the Church, not just the five-fold ministry. Ministry has nothing to do with position or professionalism. It has to do with finding out what type of anointing and gifting God has for each single person, and then fulfilling that—having been equipped, trained, and matured. Greatness in ministry is offered to the whole church. God defines greatness as "service." The leadership ministries serve in their role. Their greatness, too, is in service, not lordship or position. The congregation serves one another and their worldly neighbors. The result is a demonstration of the power of God.

THE LOVE CHAPTER: OUR CHARTER

The power of God is available to all, leadership and congregation alike. It is available from God for edification in the corporate gathering and on the streets. If we all start realizing this and start thinking this way, all God's power will be manifested that we so desire to see manifested. It is there—we just have to release it in the community, as well as in the church, by caring.

The love chapter, 1 Corinthians 13, is the church's charter. It lists the original church's purpose for existence. It stated that if all we had was the "faith to move mountains" we have missed the mark. If we are only into miracles, signs, and wonders, as great as they are, we have missed the goal of the church. If all we are into is tongues, prophecy, or words of knowledge, we are still off base. Without love all this does not ultimately profit.

If we, inspired by the gifts of the Spirit, go out and love somebody by putting our arms around them and saying "I'll walk with you through your trial," they are not going to miss that message! They are going to see the genuine thing and say, "Hey, what makes these people so different than others? What has happened to them?

Our actions will become a testimony to the life-changing power of Jesus Christ and His Gospel. As part of the church, our charity becomes the oil in the lampstand that makes the light of the Gospel burn brighter.

JUST START

I have a very nice recliner in my home. It leans way back, and it feels so good to recline in it after a hard day's work. The only bad thing is that I do not get too much accomplished while sitting there. If anything is going to be performed, I have to get up out of my recliner chair and get busy.

One night, late in the evening, I was enjoying my lovely chair, recuperating from being really tired. I had been there only a few moments when I remembered I had promised a dear sister that I would come to the hospital and pray with her. She was going to have an operation the next morning.

I did not want to get up from the chair. I was so tired. I wish I could say that I jumped right up and rushed out to minister to her. I did not. After a few more minutes, I dragged myself out of the chair, climbed into my car, and headed down to the hospital. I did not feel very powerful at all. I tried to get my spiritual motor started by praying in tongues on the way.

I walked into the hospital room, and there was this sister. "Oh Pastor, you did not need to come. God will see me through. I am okay and everything is all right." I prayed for her, blessed her, and encouraged her. Although her faith blessed me more!

As I was walking out, ready to leave, I heard in a dark little corner of the room, another little lady's voice: "Pastor, could I talk to you?"

"Sure, what's the problem?" I answered.

"I have been listening to your parishioner, and I realize I am not ready to meet God–I need to get saved. Would you pray for me that I get saved?"

I prayed for her, and she became a dear Christian who started coming to our church. What an opportunity I would have missed if I stayed in my recliner. A soul was saved! A dear sister is now heading for Heaven! An awesome divine encounter took place. For that to happen, I had to get out of my chair. I had to step out, even without feeling like it.

The Bible said, *"they went forth, and preached every where, the Lord working with them, and confirming the word with signs following"* (Mark 16:20). If we want to see miracles and the power of God released, we have to start moving. We need to get out of our four walls. Start going to our neighbors, friends, and fellow-workers, and start loving them. We need to demonstrate the love of Jesus first. The preaching or explaining will come later. Start to reach out and see what God will do through it.

RIGHTEOUS RESULTS

My wife grew up with a girlfriend in high school who was an orphan. She was my wife's best friend in high school. When they graduated, my wife lost track of her.

One day years later, my wife told me she had found out where her friend was now living, and expressed a desire to go see her. She went and discovered that her friend had gotten married to another orphan. Just two orphans striking out on the road of life by themselves. No strong family support.

My wife visited them in their home on the outskirts of town. When she returned home late that afternoon, she was extremely depressed. She revealed the squalor that they were living in. They had nothing but a little shack with two rooms, for them and five little children! They were in abject poverty. They did not have chairs to sit on. They used boxes placed around a little table, with a little forty-watt light bulb hanging over it. They did not even have a refrigerator.

She was so depressed about the poor conditions of this family. Nobody seemed to care about them. More for my wife's sake than anything, I said, "Well, maybe we can do something for them." Our church was small at that time, but I shared with the congregation on Wednesday night about this orphan friend of my wife's and how her family was in terrible need. I suggested that we could have a grocery shower. I told them that the next evening we would take them the food, so their assistance was desired.

People brought in piles of good, wonderful food—including a refrigerator to put them in! We loaded it all in a pickup truck. I remember driving out and finding this little shack just as my wife described. We walked in the dark up to the door and knocked. They opened the door, and there was my wife's friend and her husband with five small kids peeking around the corner.

I introduced myself, and told them we had brought them a little something. Two people from our congregation began to bring in the food boxes, and hardly another word was spoken. They set it all down in the little kitchen. The woman, her husband, and five little kids stood there silently, watching it all. They had never seen anything like this.

We rolled in the refrigerator, plugged it into the wall, and left saying, "God bless you!" Next Sunday morning guess who was in the church back row pew? My wife's friend, her husband, and five kids. Two weeks later, guess who came walking down the aisle to give their lives to Jesus? My wife's friend, her husband, and five kids.

It has been my privilege to marry all five of those children. They have awesome families themselves now. One of them is an Oregon State Legislator! Their children are now serving God in various churches too. All because of a few boxes of groceries.

Too often we think we have to pull teeth to convince people to come to church. Instead, you need to go to them. You serve them. You love them. You care for them. That ability and power is in your hands. The leadership ministers train, equip, and bless you in the believer's meetings so you can go forth and minister. That is being equipped to take the city, your city, for Christ. The demonstrated love of God is powerful!

God is in you. God does not stay at the altar when you leave the building Sunday morning. He abides with you, and is in you (see Matthew 28:20). Go therefore and release the power of God's love in your region. Care for your friends. Love your enemies. Do good to those who despitefully use you. People cannot resist love. They can resist everything else. They can resist doctrines, or philosophies, but love is irresistible.

That is the job of Christ's church. That is your job. And that is what the church is all about.

Believing Truth:
The Voice of Faith

Faith in God and His word begins in the heart and in the mind. It begins as an inner attitude of the soul. The mind that is enlightened by the Holy Spirit believes in, or has faith in God. That *"measure of faith"* (Romans 12:3) is given by God and is essential for beginning the Christian life.

But there is a human element in faith. As redeemed believers, we must act upon that faith to appropriate all the blessings and provisions that are reserved for us in the bank of Heaven. It does no good for the bank to be full and overflowing if we do not know how to transfer its blessings and deposit them into our lives! Unless we can appropriate the vast riches of God, spiritual and physical, we are just spinning our wheels. God's bank is full and He wants to transfer its blessings over to our lives.

God has a special way of transferring funds (blessings). He has a unique way to give us all the provisions that He has bountifully provided for us. What is that method? What is the avenue by which we can receive blessings? It is the voice of faith! Not only has God given us a heart of faith, He has given us a mouth. If we understand this, it will become the avenue by which we can receive blessings and provision. Faith has a voice.

Our words hold value; they are a product of the heart within us. As Matthew 12:34 says, *". . .for out of the abundance of the heart the mouth speaketh."* What we confess with our mouths is an indicator of the faith that is in our hearts. Because of that, our confession must faith-filled.

PROFESSION AND CONFESSION

The principles of profession and confession are repeated many times in the Bible. The writer of the epistle to the Hebrew believers noted, *"Wherefore, holy brethren, partakers of the heavenly calling, consider the Apostle and High Priest of our profession, Christ Jesus"* (Hebrews 3:1).

The Christian faith, the Christian life, involves profession and confession. It involves repeating certain beliefs so as to assimilate them into our hearts. It involves verbally expressing biblical facts. The word confession means "saying the same thing." It means repeating with our mouths what God says. Our mouths say the same thing that God utters.

IT REALLY SPEAKS!

The apostle Paul makes a wise observation in the basic doctrine book called Romans, which underlines the principle of confession, *"But the righteousness which is of faith speaketh on this wise"* (Romans 10:6a). Look closely to what is written here. God wants to give us all a key to use, not just for today, but for all our lives. Some of us have understood and used this key already. Others of us once understood this key but have laid it down. We need to realize the importance of the voice of faith.

Paul said that the righteousness of faith has a voice. It speaks. It has a vocabulary. He goes on to tell us how we are to use the vocabulary of faith. The next two verses tell us what not to say (10:6b-7), then he tells us what to say.

"Say not in thine heart, 'Who shall ascend into heaven?' (that is, to bring Christ down from above); or 'Who shall descend into the deep?' (that is to bring up Christ again from the dead.)"

No one can bring Christ down to us from heaven. He already did that on the first Christmas. He is here. He will never leave us nor forsake us. He will never orphan us. He lives in us, and manifests Himself through us. Christ in us is our hope of His manifestation on earth.

Jesus said that where two or three are gathered together, He is there in their midst (see Matthew 18:20). The righteousness of faith will speak the truth and say, "God is here. God is with me! God will never forsake me." It will speak the truth concerning God's presence.

The voice of faith also will not moan, "Who will raise up Christ from the dead? Who can deliver us from death? Who is going to take care of us now that Christ is dead?" Because Jesus Christ has been raised from the dead. This He did on the first Easter. He arose victor over death, hell, and the grave! He is ruling right now as Lord over all. He is our risen Lord!

So now, what are we to say? What does the voice of faith say? The apostle Paul continued:

"But what saith it (referring to Deuteronomy 30:14)? The word is nigh thee, even in thy mouth, and in thy heart: that is, the word of faith, which we preach; 'That if thou shalt confess with thy mouth the Lord Jesus, and shalt believe in thine heart that God hath raised him from the dead, thou shalt be saved.'" (Romans 10:8-9)

The voice of faith "confesses" the truth. It speaks the truth about Christ. It states the word that is accomplished. It is nigh. It is done. It is present. It confesses by verbally expressing the truth. If we are followers of Christ we are to be speaking the same way.

TALK THE WALK

The Bible emphasizes that we are to continue on in the faith in the same manner that we began it. *"As ye have received Christ Jesus the Lord, so walk ye in him"* (Colossians 2:6). As we have received Christ, we are to walk in that way. Our life is to be governed by the very principles and ways in which we received Him. How did we all receive Him?

We received Him by confessing Him with our mouth. *"With the mouth confession is made unto salvation."* (Romans 10:10) Notice that the word for salvation is all-encompassing. It is all-inclusive. We will have eternal life. We will prosper. We will do good. We will be healed. It has an overall implication.

"As ye have therefore received Christ Jesus. . ." (Colossians 2:6). How did we receive Him? We lifted our hands and said with our mouths, "Jesus be my Lord and Savior for I have sinned against you, Lord, and I want to receive you as my Lord and Savior; come into my heart (life)." We made a confession that we wanted Him as Lord. We made Him Lord over every area of our lives. God tells us that the manner in which we received the Lord in the beginning is the manner in which we live life. We confess with our mouths, "Jesus is Lord," daily, and we receive the blessings of His Lordship over our spirits, souls, minds, and over our bodies. In every aspect of our lives we follow this principle. Daily, in every situation, we speak the Word of the Lord. We confess what He says about our predicament. We speak what he reveals about our circumstance. We repeat what He says about us at that moment. The Christian life-style is a conversation of faith.

IDLE MOTOR-MOUTH

There is an interesting verse in the Gospel of Matthew we should examine closely.

"Out of the abundance of the heart the mouth speaketh. A good man out of the good treasure of the heart bringeth forth good things: and an evil man out of the evil treasure bringeth forth evil things. But I say unto you, That every idle word that men shall speak, they shall give account thereof in the day of judgement. For by thy words thou shalt be justified, and by thy words thou shalt be condemned." (Matthew 12:34-37)

Notice the word "idle." An automobile has a thing called an "idle." It keeps the motor running, but the car does not go anywhere. In the Bible it is used of men who are standing around in the marketplace not doing anything (see Matthew 20:3,6), and of the Cretans who were lazy (see Titus 1:12). So idle words are those which do not produce. They are not profitable. Idle talk is not constrained only to running off at the mouth, but it also includes saying things that are contrary to the word of the Lord. Any word that does not line up with what God says is idle. Anything negating the work of the cross is idle talk. Any statement that belittles the redemptive work of God over our lives is idle talk. Anything that doubts the providence of God in our lives, or the provisional love He has for us, is idle talk. Any word that comes out of our mouths and contradicts God's Word is unprofitable and idle.

TONGUE TRAITOR

If our mouths are continually contradicting the Word of God, then those "idle" words will produce an unprofitable life. Every negative word we utter as a Christian, let alone an unbeliever, will rob us of that joy. Not only will it affect us in this life and rob us of the abundant life that Jesus Christ came to give us, but it will rob us in the life to come. We will be betrayed by our own tongue!

When we stand before the Lord, God is going to ask us why we allowed our hearts to be so full of unbelief. All we are going to be able to hand to Him are lives full of wood, hay, and stubble–things that are going to be burned up. We would then spend eternity in a lesser degree than what God's plan intended for our lives.

We do not know too much about Heaven, and what is going to happen there. But we do know the Bible teaches there are degrees of reward there. There are degrees of glory. Just as there are degrees of radiance with the sun, moon, and stars (see 1 Corinthians 15:41). Some will reign over many, and some over a few. What we do and say now determines what we will reap in eternity. Our mouths here are constructing our mansions there. The Bible declares that there are going to be some who will have wasted eternity. A saved soul, but a lost reward. A complainer, a negative person, defeated all the time and never seeing the plan and glory of God in anything, will be just going to heaven by the skin of his teeth. Now, that is better than going to Hell, but I am sure we all do not want that level of existence. We want abundant entry!

EVIL SPEAKING

Because we want abundant entry, we are counseled by Paul to put away "evil speaking."

> *"Let no corrupt communication proceed out of your mouth, but only that which is good to the use of edifying, that it may minister grace unto the hearers. And grieve not the holy Spirit of God, whereby ye are sealed unto the day of redemption. Let all . . . evil speaking, be put away from you."* (Ephesians 4:29-31)

That is a stern warning! A bad mouth could grieve the Holy Spirit and that would be tragic, since the Holy Spirit seals us *"unto the day of redemption."*

Paul's counterpart in the ministry of the Gospel, the Apostle Peter, echoes these same sentiments in his epistle:

"But the Word of the Lord endureth forever. And this is the word which by the gospel is preached unto you. Wherefore laying aside all . . . evil speakings, as newborn babes, desire the sincere milk of the word." (1 Peter 1:25- 2:2)

We are to stick to the Word of God. We are to speak His Word. All other words are *"evil speakings."* We are to lay them aside and get rid of them. Instead of evil words, we are to live on the *"sincere milk of the word."* That is what edifies. That is what builds a productive life here, and one in eternity.

EXAMPLES FROM THE ANCIENTS

There are examples of the voice of faith in the Old Testament. One is a story of a fellow who really knew what it was like to be at the bottom—Jonah. We all remember the story. He refused to go to Ninevah and was thrown into the sea as he fled God's word. Then the whale swallowed him, kept him for three days and then spewed him onto the shore near Ninevah. In the end, Jonah gave God's word to the city and it repented.

He failed to agree with the revealed word of God that came to him. He refused to speak the words of God. His heart and mouth did not say the same things the will and mouth of God spoke. The consequences were disastrous.

"The waters compassed me about, even to the soul: the depth closed me round about, the weeds were wrapped about my head. I went down to the bottoms of the mountains; the earth with her bars was about me forever." (Jonah 2:5-6)

There sat Jonah, in the gastric juices of the great fish at the bottom of the sea. There is seaweed around his neck. He will be there for three days and three nights.

At first, he said nothing, but after some time he finally came to his senses. He was a little slow. It was after three days of being there in dire circumstances. He started praying, and this time he started speaking words of faith. He gave up his "idle words." He made a confession. He spoke with the vocabulary of faith. *"Yet hast thou brought up my life from corruption, O Lord my God."* Jonah 2:6b

Out of his mouth came words of faith. He spoke them before the fish spewed him onto the beach! He was not yet delivered from the depths of the ocean. Yet out of his mouth came a confession of faith.

Jonah tapped into this power principle of "the voice of faith." He began to understand the importance of voicing profitable words. The language he used determined his destiny. This was not just a mental trip or some form of positive thinking. It was faith in an objective, eternal God who is greater than circumstances. It was not because of Jonah's goodness or righteousness that he came up out of the ocean. He had failed God. It was a result of using this spiritual principle. Because of it he tapped into the resources, power, and mercy of God.

MURMURING MEN

Let's look at another example of the voice of faith found in the book of Numbers in the Old Testament. *"And the Lord spake unto Moses, saying, 'Send thou men, that they may search the land of Canaan, which I give unto the children of Israel.'"* (Numbers 13:1-2)

They went to spy out the land which God had promised to give to all the Israelites. As you know, when they came back and reported to Moses, there were two different reports. Joshua and Caleb spoke with faith. They were on the faith wavelength. *"Let us go up at once, and pos-*

sess it, for we are well able to overcome it!" (Numbers 13:30) was what Caleb affirmed. That is the voice of faith! He was saying the same thing God had said. The other ten men who went did not speak in faith. Their fate came in the desert as God did not permit any of them to enter the Promised Land.

Yes, there were giants in the land who were great obstacles. There was much work that lay ahead. Faith is not naive. Faith is not ignorant of the circumstances. But God had already said "the land which I give to you, go look it over." The language of faith is aware of the giants but it does not dwell on the negatives. The language of faith puts God's Word ahead of them always. It hones in on the Word of God. It is not unaware that there may be battles ahead. But it sees the answer as well. It focuses on the supply, the resources that will meet the needs as they crop up. Faith knows how to receive those provisions by speaking, by professing positive words of faith and trust.

METAPHORIC MIRROR

We realize that the examples given here took place several thousand years ago, before the time of Christ's incarnation. But these events were written down for our benefit. Through them, God gave the church a message. The Bible stated that things like this were written down for us upon whom the end of the age will come:

> *"Neither murmur ye, as some of them also murmured, and were destroyed by the destroyer (death angel). Now all these things happened unto them for ensamples: and they are written for our admonition, upon whom the ends of the world are come."* (1 Corinthians 10:10-11)

They are important examples of how to defeat the giants in our land. They show us how to maintain courage in an adverse society. They provide blueprints of how to gain victory over the pesky habits and character flaws in our own lives. They can help us keep fear from dominating our lives.

FEAR OR FOOD?

When the ten came back with a faithless report of the Promised Land, fear gripped the minds of the unbelieving Israelites. That fear kept them from receiving God's best for their lives and the lives of their families. It stripped them of faith in God's Word. Fear caused them to think mistakenly that they would be eaten by the giants, gobbled up by the adversary.

The voice of faith proclaimed just the opposite! *"They are bread for us"* (Numbers 14:9), declared Joshua and Caleb. Instead of being eaten alive by our problems, our problems become bread for us. They provide us with nourishment. Our adverse circumstances, in fact, give us an opportunity to increase our strength! With God's help, our battles, giants, and troubles are occasions to increase maturity and bring about extensions of God's kingdom.

When we are hedged in on every side and feel like we are at the bottom of the barrel, then it is time to speak with the voice of faith. Caleb and Joshua said their problems were bread. Our problems can be as well.

PAUL'S REAL LIFE EXPERIENCE

The apostle Paul was not just talking off the top of his head when he underscored this truth. He really knew about giants. And wolves. And tyrants. And roaring lions. He knew adversity. He had problems—lots of them. Paul was not some slick marble statue, gilded with gold and inset with rare jewels in a pristine cathedral for people to admire when they came in their Sunday best. Paul was a mortal man, an earthen vessel. But he knew this important truth:

> *"But we have this treasure in earthen vessels, that the excellency of the power may be of God, and not of us. We are troubled on every side, yet not distressed; we are perplexed, but not in despair; persecuted, but not forsaken; cast down, but not destroyed; always bearing about in the body the dying of the Lord Jesus, that the life also of Jesus might be made manifest in our body. We having the same spirit of faith, according as it is written, 'I believed, and therefore have I spoken.' We also believe, and therefore speak."* (2 Corinthians 4:7-10,13)

Paul was troubled, even as we are. He was perplexed, even as we become perplexed. He was under a lot of pressure, even as we often have pressure.

But we are not in despair. We are not forsaken. We are not destroyed. The war is won, and once in a while we get a good hard bump, but we are not going to go down. *"Always bearing about in [our] body the dying of the Lord Jesus."* We suffer the same taunts and persecution Jesus did.

The voice of faith enables us to go through crisis hours and not crumble. When we speak the vocabulary of faith we will not fold and whimper like a beaten pup. We go through crisis hours with our heads held up in the air trusting God. Those who do not know the Lord will see our strength and stand in amazement. They are going to realize there is something working in us that is not working in them. The Christ-life will shine through, bringing many to salvation.

ALL THINGS

Paul continued his encouragement by stating that *"all things are for your sakes, that the abundant grace might through the thanksgiving of many rebound to the glory of God."* (2 Corinthians 4:15). Every time we go through a battle, face adversity, or enter a crisis, all things are for our sakes.

If we go through adversity with the voice of faith declaring the Word of the Lord, as God wants us to, that circumstance will work for our benefit. God will accomplish some good out of it.

If we go the other route—whimper and complain, doubt and criticize God, and say, "I do not have any hope for tomorrow, it is just a hopeless situation," our words of doubt will have a negative effect. We failed to see that every adversity is bread, and every battle is our opportunity to mature, shine, and allow Christ in us to manifest.

All things happen for our sakes. If we keep the voice of faith on our lips, those things will only help us.

AFFIRMATIONS

The New Testament Apostles understood the voice of faith principle. Over and over again in his letters, Paul uses the phrase "this is a faithful saying." He recognized there are some things that bear repeating. There are some words of encouragement that need to be vocalized. Once he wrote this, *"This is a faithful saying, and these things I will that thou affirm constantly"* (Titus 3:8).

We need to affirm constantly. Speak out daily. Vocalize with assurance often. Repeat these faithful sayings over and over.

It would be good for us in a practical way to sit down and list some "faithful sayings," some affirmations of our faith, just as the early Christians sat down and wrote "the Apostles creed" to repeat over and over again. Doing so will establish faith in our hearts and minds.

Personal affirmations are important too. As a young man just starting in the ministry, I remember being buffeted by circumstances, areas
of doubt, and insecurity. I sat down and looked up Scriptures from the
Word of God that revealed facts about me as a believer. I repeated them
over and over again. I agreed with what the Word of the Lord said
about me. It brought stability to my life. I affirmed what God was doing
in my life, instead of listening to doubts and unbelief.

Perhaps, as a matter of practical overcoming in each of our lives, it
would be good for us all to write out affirmations from the Word of God.
I am sure God would be delighted in this. Here are some examples:

- *I am loved*   1 John 3:1; John 15:9

- *I am forgiven*   1 John 1:9; Luke 7:47

- *I am restored*   Psalm 23:1-3

- *I am a new creation*   2 Corinthians 5:17

- *I am understood*   Hebrews 4:15-16

- *I am complete*   Colossians 2:9-10

- *I am important*   Luke 12:6; Isaiah 49:15-16

- *I am destined*   1 Corinthians 15:51-53

- *I am free*   Romans 8:2; John 8:31-36

- *I am secure*   Romans 8:31

- *I am a conqueror*   Romans 8:37

Say these things out loud and encourage one another with words
of faith. Let your voice be heard. It would not hurt if you started each
morning with such affirmations. Look in your mirror at home, lift up
your chin, straighten your shoulders, throw back your head. Lift up
your voice and speak with confidence. "I am a child of God!" Say it with
a voice of faith. Say it until you really believe it. Say it until your wife
believes you. Say it until your children believe you. Say it until Satan

believes you and trembles. Say it until the angels look down over the bannister of heaven to see who is talking. Say it until God hearkens. Until God hears you, and takes note! Say it until the world wakes up and listens.

This is God's intention for the church. This is God's plan for the church. People moving ahead, with full assurance, speaking with the voice of faith.

"Therefore, brethren, stand fast, and hold the traditions which you have been taught, whether by word, or our epistle. Now our Lord Jesus Christ himself, and God, even our Father, which hath loved us, and hath given us everlasting consolation and good hope through grace, comfort your hearts, and stablish you in every good word and work." (2 Thessalonians 2:15-17)

Those congregations that in unison speak the word of faith will prosper. God will take heed! The prophet Malachi noted, *"Then they that feared the Lord spake often one to another, and the Lord hearkened, and heard it, and a book of remembrance was written before him for them . . ."* (Malachi 3:16). What do you think they were saying? Were they complaining? No! Undoubtedly they were all encouraging one another, speaking the word of faith! They were speaking "every good word." These are the kind of people who are overcomers.

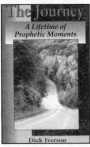